BASIC/NOT BORING
SOCIAL STUDIES SKILLS

MIDDLE GRADE BOOK OF SOCIAL STUDIES TESTS

Series Concept & Development
by Imogene Forte & Marjorie Frank

Illustrations by Kathleen Bullock

Incentive Publications, Inc.
Nashville, Tennessee

About the cover:
Bound resist, or tie dye, is the most ancient known method of fabric surface design. The brilliance of the basic tie dye design on this cover reflects the possibilities that emerge from the mastery of basic skills.

Cover art by Mary Patricia Deprez, dba Tye Dye Mary®
Cover design by Marta Drayton and Joe Shibley
Edited by Jean K. Signor

ISBN 0-86530-493-9

PRINTED IN THE UNITED STATES OF AMERICA
www.incentivepublications.com

TABLE OF CONTENTS

Inside the Middle Grade Book of Social Studies Tests 7

How to Use the Middle Grade Book of Social Studies Tests 8

WORLD UNDERSTANDINGS 10–23

Test # 1 Social & Cultural Concepts & Relationships 12

Test # 2 World Cultures 18

Test # 3 Economics 24

WORLD GEOGRAPHY 30–55

World Geography Skills Checklists 30

Test # 1 Geographical Features 33

Test # 2 World Regions 38

Test # 3 Important Places & Spaces 42

Test # 4 U.S. Geography 48

Test # 5 Human Geography 52

MAP SKILLS 56–71

Map Skills Checklists 56

Test # 1 Map Tools & Resources 58

Test # 2 Directions, Distances, & Locations 62

Test # 3 Finding Information on Maps 66

WORLD HISTORY 72–105

World History Skills Checklists 72

Test # 1 Major Eras & Events 75

Test # 2 People, Places, & Organizations 82

Test # 3 Ancient World History 88

Test # 4 Medieval & Modern History Through 1900 94

Test # 5 Modern History Since 1900 100

World Understandings Skills Checklists 10

U. S. HISTORY 106–133

    U.S. History Skills Checklists 106

    Test # 1 Major Eras & Events 109

    Test # 2 People, Places, & Organizations 114

    Test # 3 Early History (through 1800) 120

    Test # 4 19th Century History 124

    Test # 5 Modern History Since 1900 128

U. S. GOVERNMENT & CITIZENSHIP 134–152

    U.S. Government & Citizenship Skills Checklists 134

    Test # 1 Key U.S. Documents 136

    Test # 2 Government Structure & Function 140

    Test # 3 Officials, Agencies, & Institutions 146

    Test # 4 U.S. Citizenship 150

KEEPING TRACK OF SKILLS 153

    Student Progress Record 154

    Class Progress Record
        (World Understandings, World Geography) 155

    Class Progress Records
        (Map Skills, World History) 156

    Class Progress Record
        (U.S. History, U.S Government and Citizenship) 157

    Good Skill Sharpeners for Social Studies 158

ANSWER KEYS 161

    World Understandings Answer Keys 162

    World Geography Answer Keys 164

    Map Skills Answer Keys 166

    World History Answer Keys 168

    U. S. History Answer Keys 171

    U.S. Government and Citizenship Answer Keys 174

INSIDE THE
MIDDLE GRADE BOOK OF SOCIAL STUDIES TESTS

"I wish I had a convenient, fast way to assess basic skills and standards."
"If only I had a way to find out what my students already know about social studies!"
"If only I had a good way to find out what my students have learned!"
"How can I tell if my students are ready for state assessments?"
"It takes too long to create my own tests on the units I teach."
"The tests that come with my textbooks are too long and too dull."
"I need tests that cover all the skills on a topic—not just a few here and there."

This is what teachers tell us about their needs for testing materials. If you, too, are looking for quality, convenient materials that will help you gauge how well students are moving along towards mastering basic skills and standards—look no further. This is a book of tests such as you've never seen before! It's everything you've wanted in a group of ready-made social studies assessments for middle grade students.

- The tests are student-friendly. One glance through the book and you will see why. Students will be surprised that it's a test at all! The pages are inviting and fun. A clever rat and a cool cat tumble over the pages, leading students through social studies challenges and problems. Your students will not groan when you pass out these tests. They'll want to stick with them all the way to the end to see what's happening with the STOP sign this time!

- The tests are serious. Do not be fooled by the catchy characters and visual appeal! These are serious, thorough assessments of basic content. As a part of the BASIC/Not Boring Skills Series, they give broad coverage of skills with a flair that makes them favorites of teachers and kids.

- The tests cover all the basic skill areas for social studies. There are 25 tests within 6 areas: world understandings, world geography, map skills, world history, U.S. history, and U.S. government and citizenship.

- The tests are ready to use. In convenient and manageable sizes, each test covers a skill area (such as economics, ancient world history, or human geography) that should be assessed. Just give the pages to an individual student, or make copies for the entire class. Answer keys (included in back) are easy to find and easy to use.

- Skills are clearly identified. You can see exactly which skills are tested by reviewing the list of skills provided with each category of tests.

HOW TO USE THE
MIDDLE GRADE BOOK OF SOCIAL STUDIES TESTS

Each test can be used in many different ways. Here are a few:

- as a pre-test to see what a student knows or can do on a certain social studies topic
- as a post-test to find out how well students have mastered a content or skill area
- as a review to check up on student mastery of standards or readiness for state assessments
- as a survey to provide direction for your present or future instruction
- as an instructional tool to guide students through a review of a lesson
- with one student in an assessment or tutorial setting
- with a small group of students for assessment or instruction
- with a whole class for end-of-unit assessment

The book provides you with tools for using the tests effectively and keeping track of how students are progressing on skills or standards:

- 25 Tests on the Topics You Need: These are grouped according to broad topics within social studies. Each large grouping has three or more sub-tests. Tests are clearly labeled with subject area and specific topic.

- Skills Checklists Correlated to Test Items: At the beginning of each group of tests, you'll find a list of the skills covered. (For instance, pages 10 and 11 hold lists of skills for the three tests on world understandings.) Each skill is matched with the exact test items assessing that skill. If a student misses an item on the test, you'll know exactly which skill needs sharpening.

- Student Progress Records: Page 154 holds a reproducible form that can be used to track individual student achievement on all the tests in this book. Make a copy of this form for each student, and record the student's test scores and areas of instructional need.

- Class Progress Records: Pages 156–158 hold reproducible forms for keeping track of a whole class. You can record the dates that tests are given, and keep comments about what you learned from that test as well as notes for further instructional needs.

- Reference for Skill Sharpening Activities: Pages 159–160 describe a program of appealing exercises designed to teach, strengthen, or reinforce basic social studies skills and content. The skills covered in these books are correlated to national curriculum standards and the standards for many states.

- Answer Keys: An easy-to-use answer key is provided for each of the 25 tests (see pages 162–176).

THE MIDDLE GRADE SOCIAL STUDIES TESTS

World Understandings Skills Checklists 10–11

   3 World Understandings Tests 12–29

World Geography Skills Checklists 30–32

   5 World Geography Tests 33–55

Map Skills Checklists 56–57

   3 Map Skills Tests 58–71

World History Skills Checklists 72–74

   5 World History Tests 75–105

U.S. History Skills Checklists 106–108

   5 U.S. History Tests 109–133

U.S. Government & Citizenship Skills Checklists 134–135

   4 U.S. Government & Citizenship Tests 136–152

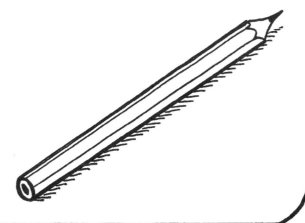

World Understandings Skills Checklists

World Understandings Test # 1:

CULTURAL CONCEPTS & RELATIONSHIPS

Test Location: pages 12–17

Skill	*Test Items*
Identify expressions of culture	1
Identify ways culture is gained and transmitted	2, 4
Identify factors that influence the development of culture	3, 5
Define cultural concepts and terms	6–23
Identify features of a culture's economic and political systems	24, 25
Show understanding of the concept of a social group	26
Identify roles played by individuals in social groups	27–28
Identify functions and purposes of social institutions	29–38
Identify needs that are similar in all cultures	39
Describe the function of technology in a culture	40
Discriminate between cultural concepts such as taboo, tradition, value, role, sects, clans, customs, and rituals	41–47
Identify examples of a cultural response to the physical or social environment	48, 53
Identify examples of ways different cultures meet human needs in similar and different ways	49–50
Identify ways that culture is transmitted through art or traditions	51, 54
Identify reasons for movement or migration within a culture	52
Identify ways that technology changes cultures	55

Middle Grade Book of Social Studies Tests

World Understandings Test # 2:

WORLD CULTURES

Test Location: pages 18–23

Skill	*Test Items*
Recognize some general characteristics of a sampling of world cultures	1–7
Recognize characteristics of some of the world's major religions	8–16
Show understandings of some expressions and influences of culture, as related to specific examples in world cultural situations	17–24
Identify characteristics of different government and political systems	25–34
Show understanding of some aspects of world population	35–37
Recognize characteristics and aspects of various world cultural regions	39–50

World Understandings Test # 3:

ECONOMICS

Test Location: pages 24–29

Skill	*Test Items*
Identify ways to define an economic system	1
Distinguish among different types of economic systems	2–4
Understand and define a nation's GNP and balance of trade	5–6
Show understanding that economic choices have costs and benefits	7–8
Identify characteristics of developing and developed economies	9–10
Identify institutions that regulate economic activities	11
Show understanding of the concept of scarcity as a factor in economic choice	12
Show understanding of the reasons products are valued in a society	13
Identify features of a market economy and a welfare state	14–15
Show understanding of the relationships between supply, demand, prices, and production	16–17, 19
Show understanding of the effects of competition on prices and services	18
Identify incentives for economic choices	20–21
Identify purposes of the Federal Reserve System	22
Show understanding of the meaning of economic terms and concepts	23–45

CULTURAL CONCEPTS & RELATIONSHIPS

Name _____

Possible Correct Answers: 55

Date _____

Your Correct Answers: _____

1. A student wants to learn about a culture. He'll examine these aspects of the society. Which one of these is LEAST LIKELY to give him insight into the aspects of the culture?

    a. the social organizations

    b. the recreational activities

    c. social and religious traditions

    d. the economic system

    e. the people's need for food and water

    f. governmental structure

    g. ways of relating to the environment

2. Culture has been transmitted to children in a family. Which of these has probably been LEAST important in transmitting culture?

    a. the language of their country

    b. paintings and other works of art

    c. the media

    d. weather patterns

    e. holiday celebrations

    f. religious practices of their family

    g. music and other forms of entertainment

    h. family traditions

3. Which of these factors would probably have the LEAST influence on the development of a culture?

a. the average height of the adults

b. the climate of the area

c. the resources available to the people

d. the topography of the area

4. How does a person gain culture?

    a. It is learned.

    b. People are born knowing the culture.

    c. People choose a culture when they become adults.

5. Which factor is most responsible for changes in cultures?

    a. weather disasters

    b. war

    c. disease or famine

    d. diffusion

A student has matched explanations to some concepts about culture.
How well does she really understand these terms? Check her answers.
Cross out any incorrect answers and write the correct letter instead.

____6. civilization

____7. society

____8. culture

____9. religion

____10. ethnicity

____11. economy

____12. diversity

____13. technology

____14. government

____15. indigenous

____16. history

____17. assimilation

____18. dialects

____19. immigrant

____20. diffusion

____21. socialization

____22. nomads

____23. descendants

a. the way people in a group use resources to meet their needs

b. native to an area

c. the process of learning one's culture

d. an organized society that has made advances in arts and sciences

e. regional variations in a spoken language

f. a system of faith and beliefs in a god or gods

g. people who share a common ancestry

h. the shared past of a group

i. a system or group that makes decisions for the people in a social group, state, or nation

j. a group of people who share a common culture

k. variety of cultural backgrounds

l. the racial, religious, or cultural background of an individual or group

m. someone who comes to live in a country from another country

n. a group that travels for trade, work, or food

o. the spread of new ideas through a culture

p. the tools, skills, and resources of a group

q. the total way of life of a group of people

r. the process by which an individual or group adopts ways of another culture

Middle Grade Book of Social Studies Tests

Cultural Concepts & Relationships

page 3 of 6

24. The student wants to learn about the economic system of a culture. Which question would be LEAST helpful to ask?

    a. What do the people like to eat?

    b. Who decides what goods are produced?

    c. How are goods or resources shared?

    d. How do goods get from one place to another?

    e. How are workers rewarded for their labor?

25. The student wants to learn about the political system of a culture. Which question would be LEAST helpful to ask?

    a. Who has the power in the society?

    b. How are the leaders chosen?

    c. What rights do citizens have?

    d. What are the responsibilities of the citizens?

    e. How many different languages are spoken?

26. At some time this week, Ramon was a part of each of these groups. Which of them could be described as social groups? *(Circle all that apply.)*

    a. his family   d. people in line at a drug store

    b. his soccer team   e. members of a computer club

    c. people riding a subway   f. his seventh grade math class

27. Angela Brown is the vice president of an advertising agency. She has three children and a husband. On weekends, she teachers Sunday School at her church and volunteers as an emergency rescue worker. When she takes a big pot of spaghetti to her aged mother on Saturday, what social role is she fulfilling?

    a. mother

    b. vice president

    c. daughter

    d. Sunday School teacher

    e. rescue worker

28. Officer Jones is a police officer and a father of two children. He coaches a soccer team on weekends and bowls on a neighborhood bowling team. When he helps a boy next door with soccer drills (the boy is NOT a member of his team), what social role is he fulfilling?

    a. father

    b. neighbor

    c. police officer

    d. soccer coach

    e. bowling team member

Name

14

Middle Grade Book of Social Studies Tests   Copyright ©2001 by Incentive Publications, Inc., Nashville, TN.

What are the purposes or functions of these social institutions? For each one, write the letter of at least one choice from the chart. (Many of the examples will have more than one function.)

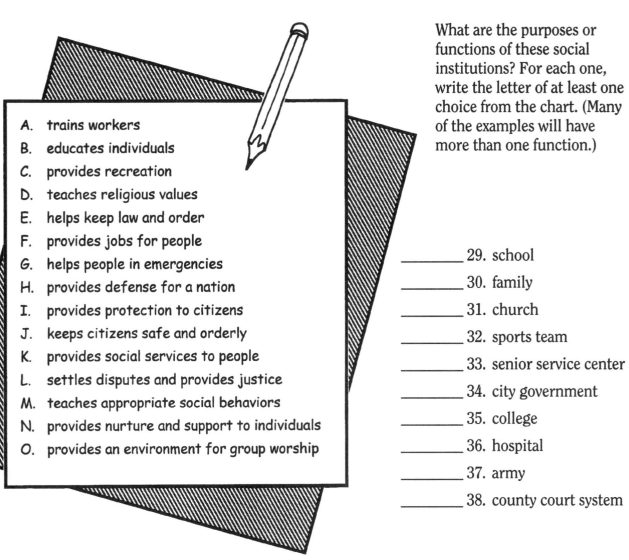

A. trains workers
B. educates individuals
C. provides recreation
D. teaches religious values
E. helps keep law and order
F. provides jobs for people
G. helps people in emergencies
H. provides defense for a nation
I. provides protection to citizens
J. keeps citizens safe and orderly
K. provides social services to people
L. settles disputes and provides justice
M. teaches appropriate social behaviors
N. provides nurture and support to individuals
O. provides an environment for group worship

_____ 29. school
_____ 30. family
_____ 31. church
_____ 32. sports team
_____ 33. senior service center
_____ 34. city government
_____ 35. college
_____ 36. hospital
_____ 37. army
_____ 38. county court system

39. Which needs are the same for humans in any culture?
(Circle all that apply.)

a. the need for a new car
b. the need for shelter
c. the need for safety
d. the need for food
e. the need to have money saved
f. the need for social relationships
g. the need for fast transportation
h. the need for health insurance

40. Which is a major function of technology in a culture?
a. It gives people more ways to make use of environmental resources.
b. It provides the society a way to learn their language.
c. It gives the society a system of law and justice.
d. It gives the society a way to pass on important cultural values.

Name _____ **15** _____

Choose the answer that will correctly complete the sentence.

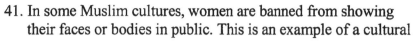

41. In some Muslim cultures, women are banned from showing their faces or bodies in public. This is an example of a cultural
    a. taboo.   b. change.   c. role.   d. ritual.

42. For many generations, Hindu marriages were arranged by the parents of a boy and girl long before they became old enough to marry. This practice, followed less often today, is an example of a cultural
    a. taboo.   b. tradition.   c. law.   d. religious belief.

43. In some Hispanic cultures, families believe it is important to have many children. Members of such a culture may feel sorry for a family that has no children or only one child. The importance of large families is an example of a cultural
    a. taboo.   b. adaptation.   c. value.   d. tradition.

44. The family of a young Scottish boy belongs to a group of families who are descended from a common ancestor. This group of families is an example of a
    a. sect.   b. clan.   c. tribe.   d. club.

45. Gina and Anthony are neighbors. Both belong to families that attend Christian protestant churches. Gina's family belongs to a Presbyterian church. Anthony's family belongs to a Baptist church. These two churches are examples of different
    a. gangs.   b. clans.   c. sects.   d. tribes.   e. societies.

46. In a part of Thailand, Akha women wear beautiful headdresses decorated with silver, feathers, coins, and beads. As they grow older, they add decorations until the headdresses become larger and heavier. This behavior is an example of a(n)
    a. value.   b. custom.   c. rule.   d. assimilation.

47. At Sabrina's church, communion is served to the church members every Sunday. This practice is an example of a
    a. law.   b. ritual.   c. value.   d. role.

Name _____

Middle Grade Book of Social Studies Tests   Copyright ©2001 by Incentive Publications, Inc., Nashville, TN.

Read this list. It contains descriptions of some cultural behaviors or traditions.
Choose ONE of these examples from the list to answer each question below.
(There may be more than one possible answer for some questions.)

A. The hunting has been poor and members of the group are getting short on food.

B. The people of Indonesia are scattered over 13,000 islands, and therefore, 150 different languages and dialects are spoken in the country.

C. Families in most cultures provide care for babies and small children.

D. A North American Indian tribe carved a huge totem pole with a series of symbols picturing events in the tribe's history.

E. Each Thanksgiving, members of Julie's community reenact the landing of the Pilgrims at Plymouth Rock.

F. Many families in Hong Kong live on houseboats in the harbor because there is little room for more houses on the land.

G. Members of the Intuit culture in the Arctic no longer have to rely on dogsleds for transportation across the icy land. Now they travel across the long, icy distances more quickly with airplanes and snowmobiles.

H. A father in Belgium works to earn money to pay rent for his family's apartment, while a father in central Africa builds a mud-brick home for his family.

Which item from the list is an example of . . .

_____ 48. a culture's response to the physical environment (land or climate)?

_____ 49. how different cultures meet a human need in a similar way?

_____ 50. how different cultures meet a human need in different ways?

_____ 51. a way that culture is transmitted through a tradition?

_____ 52. a reason for the movement or migration of a group?

_____ 53. a culture's response to the social environment?

_____ 54. a way that culture is transmitted through art?

_____ 55. a way that technology changes cultures?

Name _____

Middle Grade Book of Social Studies Tests

WORLD CULTURES

Name _____

Date _____

Possible Correct Answers: 50

Your Correct Answers: _____

1. While traveling to study cultures around the world, Aristotle meets a Berber woman carrying water from a well. Most likely, he has met this woman in

    a. the rainforest of Brazil.

    b. a desert in North Africa.

    c. the mountains of West Asia.

2. Aristotle visits with some Inuits whose family has a long history of hunting seals and caribou. He is probably on

    a. an Arctic tundra.

    b. a New Zealand beach.

    c. a river in Indonesia.

3. In what cultural region is Aristotle most likely to meet many people of mestizo descent (a mixture of Spanish and Indian)?

    a. the middle east

    b. Central America and Mexico

    c. Southern Europe

4. He visits with some Bantu people. This group of people forms a large number of ethnic groups in

    a. Southeast Asia.

    b. Northern Asia.

    c. Southeast Africa.

5. When he travels an area of the world with millions of people who speak the Arabic language and follow the Islamic faith, Aristotle is most likely in

    a. Latin America.

    b. North Africa or the Middle East.

    c. Australia.

6. He enjoys listening to a group singing reggae music, inspired by Rastafarian faith and influenced by African rhythms. He is probably in

    a. the Caribbean Islands.

    b. Northern Europe.

    c. the Far East.

7. Where is he most likely to meet many people of an aboriginal culture?

    a. North America

    b. Australia

    c. India

Some of the world's major religions are described.
Match the name of the religion for each example. (Write the letter.)

A. Islam

B. Taoism

C. Sikhism

D. Judaism

E. Shinto

F. Confucianism

G. Christianity

H. Buddhism

I. Hinduism

_____ 8. A family in East Asia follows the teachings of one of China's greatest philosophers. Their religion is a set of rules for behavior. The importance of strong family ties is a main value. In addition, their religion values learning, honesty, respect for others, and hard work.

_____ 9. Another family follows a different religion of East Asia. This religion teaches that people should calmly accept whatever happens to them-that they should leave things the way they are, and not try to change them.

_____ 10. A family in the Middle East follows the teachings of the prophet Muhammad. They believe in one god, called Allah. Their holy book is the Koran.

_____ 11. A Hebrew family believes in one God, whom they call Yahweh, or Jehovah. They follow the laws set in the books of Moses in the Bible's Old Testament, and in the Torah.

_____ 12. Another family believes that Jesus Christ is the son of God. They follow the teachings of the Bible's Old Testament and New Testament. They worship one God.

_____ 13. A family in Asia follows a religion based on the teachings of Siddhartha Gautama. They believe that selfishness or a desire for things causes humans to suffer. The followers practice physical and spiritual discipline to gain wisdom and inner peace.

_____ 14. A family in Japan follows the oldest Japanese religion. They believe that spirits dwell in natural living things and objects, and have great reverence for their ancestors.

_____ 15. A family in India believes that all living things have a soul, and all life is holy. They also believe that the soul is reborn into a new body after death. This belief is called reincarnation. The goal of the religion is to eventually release the soul from the life-death cycle into eternity.

_____ 16. A family in northern India follows a religion that was founded in the late 1400s, blending together some elements of two other religions: Hinduism and Islam.

Middle Grade Book of Social Studies Tests

Circle the best answer.

17. Some groups of people have left their home region to find better jobs or to find a more affordable place to live. Some leave their home countries to get away from religious intolerance, political oppression, crime, or war. These are all reasons for the _____ of groups.
    a. blending
    b. migration
    c. conflict
    d. growth

18. The Mexico City area of Mexico is a large, continuous sprawl of towns, cities, and suburbs. This is an example of a
    a. rural area.   b. megalopolis.   c. nation.   d. county.

19. A strong sense of national identity and zealous pride in the country sometimes leads to intense conflicts between groups. This sense is called
    a. separatism.   b. isolationism.   c. colonialism.   d. nationalism.

20. In 1948, some people who believed they had a reason to belong together, formed a government, and created the _____ of Israel.
    a. alliance   b. nation   c. continent   d. colony

21. Which would NOT be an example of the fine arts of a Southeast Asian culture?
    a. pottery   b. music   c. the literature   d. mining equipment
    e. dances   f. paintings

22. The land, people, and economies of many countries in the world have been torn apart by wars between the citizens of the same country. This is called
    a. civil war.   b. international   c. world war.   d. famine.
                              conflict.

23. The way of life in the United States blends traditions and other traits from many cultures. This is an example of
    a. bigotry.   b. cultural pluralism.   c. nationalism.   d. culture shock.

24. Throughout history, many cultural groups in regions of Africa believed that they should be allowed to govern themselves. This struggle, which has led to many wars, is a fight for
    a. peace.   b. colonialism.   c. autonomy.   d. migration.

Name _____

20

Choose the correct government description for each blank.
Write the letter.

A. empire
B. republic
C. parliamentary government
D. anarchy
E. constitutional monarchy
F. dictatorship
G. confederacy
H. constitutional government
I. monarchy
J. commonwealth

25. In a(n) _____, one ruler (who has not usually inherited the power) has total control over the nation. Often the nation is controlled by force.

26. In a(n) ____, a group of officials (who are not necessarily elected) make the laws. Often the leader is a prime minister who gains the position because his/her political party won the election.

27. A(n) _____ is a nation in which citizens elect officials to represent them in government.

28. _____ describes a system of no government or organized authority.

29. In a(n) _____, the power of the person or group running the government is limited by a constitution.

30. A(n) ____ is a political organization where states combine for some purpose but each state retains its sovereignty.

31. A(n) ____ is a self-governing territory.

32. A(n) ____ is a group of nations or territories ruled by one ruler.

33. A(n) _____ is a nation ruled by a supreme sovereign such as an emperor, king, or queen. Usually the sovereign inherited the position.

34. In a(n) ___, the government is headed by a king or queen, but a separate constitutional government rules the country.

Middle Grade Book of Social Studies Tests

35. Which of these groups of facts about the world is most accurate?

    a. about 6 billion people, 150 countries, and 3000 different languages.

    b. about 6 million people, 150 countries and 200 different languages.

    c. about 1 billion people, 500 countries, and 50 different languages.

    d. about 60 billion people, 100 countries and 300 different languages.

36. The largest percentage of population in the USA and European countries is found

    a. in isolated settlements throughout the countries.

    b. in larger cities throughout the countries.

    c. in the countryside.

    d. on the ocean.

37. The largest percentage of population in Africa and Southeast Asia is found

    a. in isolated settlements along the coastlines.

    b. in a few large cities.

    c. in the countryside.

    d. on the ocean.

38. Which is true of both Canada and the United States?

    a. Both countries have English as the only official language.

    b. They both have free enterprise economies.

    c. They both have a president as the head of the government.

    d. The economy is based on agriculture.

39. Which is not true of recent life in Latin America?

    a. Many Latin American governments have suffered from political instability.

    b. In recent history, several countries have been in the control of military juntas.

    c. The region has a rich heritage of art and music.

    d. Most of the thriving cities are found in coastal areas.

    e. The economies are most strongly based on industry and manufacturing.

40. Most of the best land in Central America is used for

    a. cities.

    b. subsistence farming.

    c. tourist resorts.

    d. large coffee, banana, or sugarcane plantations.

41. In recent history, tourism in Cuba has been most hampered by

    a. hurricane destruction of the beaches.

    b. a poor economy.

    c. the Cuban revolution and Communist control of the country.

    d. difficult transportation routes.

Choose an answer from the list.

Southeast Asia

Antarctica   CHINA

Latin America

North America

Sub-Saharan Africa

Oceania   Middle East

Western Europe

Eastern Europe

United Nations   NATO

North Africa

European Community

Turkey   Iraq

English

Yiddish   Pakistan

French   Arabic

the caste system

feudalism   apartheid

Malaysia

_____42. Region where most countries were colonies of European nations until about 40 years ago

_____43. Region of the world known for rich oil production, as well as conflicts over boundaries and control of religious sites

_____44. Region of no permanent human settlements

_____45. An organization formed to promote free trade and transportation among European nations

_____46. The official language spoken in Lebanon, Syria, Jordan, Algeria, Kuwait, Egypt, Iraq, Yemen, Sudan, Morocco, Tunisia, and Libya

_____47. Region where strong communist control has given way to new nations and new democracies in the late 20th century

_____48. The country created as a homeland for members of India's Muslim minority

_____49. a system of laws used to separate people of different races in South Africa

_____50. region of over one billion people, where life changed radically in almost every way after the Cultural Revolution of 1949

Name _____

Middle Grade Book of Social Studies Tests

ECONOMICS

Name _____   Possible Correct Answers: 45

Date _____   Your Correct Answers: _____

1. Three basic questions help to define an economic system.
   Which questions are they? Circle three.

   > **A. Which goods and services will be produced?**
   >
   > **B. How many political parties are in the government?**
   >
   > **C. How will the goods and services be produced?**
   >
   > **D. How stable are the banks and other financial services?**
   >
   > **E. Which buyers in the economy have the most money?**
   >
   > **F. Who will consume the goods and services?**

2. An economic system in which most businesses are owned and operated by individuals, with
   relatively little government control, is a

   a. free enterprise system.   b. socialistic system.   c. mixed economic system.

3. An economic system in which some industry is government controlled and others are controlled
   by private individuals is a

   a. free enterprise system.   b. socialistic system.   c. mixed economic system.

4. An economy in which the government basically runs the economy and controls the natural
   resources, and where there is an attempt to spread the wealth equally among all citizens, is a

   a. free enterprise system.   b. socialistic system.   c. mixed economic system.

5. What is meant by a nation's balance of trade?

   a. the difference between its standards of living and that of its neighboring countries

   b. the total value of its economy's worth divided by the number of people in the country

   c. the difference between the total value of that nation's imports and exports

6. Which of these is the main indicator used to measure a nation's wealth?

   a. the CPI   b. the Dow-Jones average   c. the GNP   d. the tax rate

7. Which statement about economic choices is true?

    a. Every economic choice has costs and benefits.

    b. Most, but not all, economic choices have benefits

    c. Some economic choices have no costs.

8. Milanni considers buying a motorcycle that will cost her $80 a month for a year with no interest. She also considers a newer cycle that has more power and fancier features. This would cost her $95 a month for two years with interest. She chooses the older cycle.

    A. What are the costs of this choice (What does she give up when she makes this choice)?

_____

    B. What are the benefits of this choice?_____

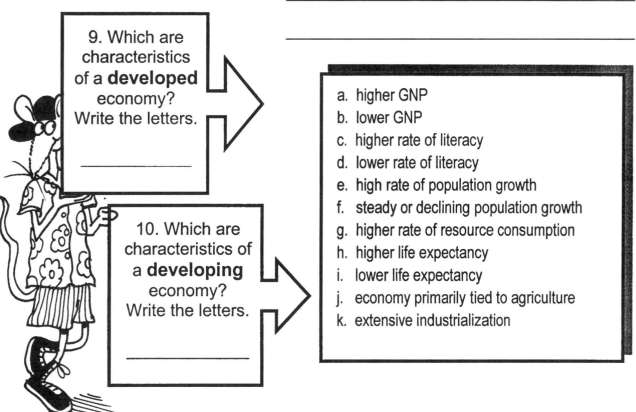

9. Which are characteristics of a **developed** economy? Write the letters.

_____

10. Which are characteristics of a **developing** economy? Write the letters.

_____

    a. higher GNP
    b. lower GNP
    c. higher rate of literacy
    d. lower rate of literacy
    e. high rate of population growth
    f. steady or declining population growth
    g. higher rate of resource consumption
    h. higher life expectancy
    i. lower life expectancy
    j. economy primarily tied to agriculture
    k. extensive industrialization

11. Which of the following institutions would play a part in regulating or monitoring the United States economic activities? (Circle all that apply.)

    a. the Federal Reserve

    b. the Federal Trade Commission

    c. the Federal Bureau of Investigation

    d. the Department of Justice

    e. the Milk Marketing Board

Name _____

25

12. Which statements below are true? (Circle one or more answers.)

    a. The scarcity of resources influences personal and national economic decisions.

    b. Most human, capital, and natural resources are unlimited.

    c. Every economic choice has both benefits and costs.

    d. Positive and negative influences affect the economic choices people make.

13. In a market economy, a product has value when it is (Circle one or more answers.)

    (a. scarce)   (b. plentiful)   (c. useful)   (d. desired)   (e. undesirable)

14. Which benefit would probably NOT be available to citizens in a welfare state?

    a. a government that takes responsibility for the well-being of all its citizens

    b. free or very affordable national health care

    c. a guaranteed low tax rate

    d. government-provided child care

    e. unemployment insurance

15. In a market economy, what is the main incentive for producing goods?

    a. to provide needed services or goods for all citizens

    b. to make profit

    c. to add to a healthy economy for the nation

    d. to promote economic equity

16. What happens when the supply of blue jeans is greater than the demand for them?

    a. People stop buying jeans.

    b. The price of jeans goes up.

    c. The price of jeans goes down.

    d. The manufacturers produce more jeans.

17. If prices for automobiles increase, what would be the expected result?

    a. Buyers would buy fewer autos and manufacturers would increase auto production.

    b. Buyers would buy more autos and manufacturers would increase auto production.

    c. Buyers would buy more autos and manufacturers would decrease auto production.

    d. Buyers would buy fewer autos and manufacturers would decrease auto production.

Name _____

Middle Grade Book of Social Studies Tests

18. Last summer, Janna ate a peach sundae every day. This summer, peaches are scarce because of bad weather during the growing season. What kind of prices can Janna expect when she goes to buy peaches?

a. higher prices

b. lower prices

c. prices about the same

19. For years, an air route between Orange City and Blue City has been serviced only by ColorJet Airlines. Two new airlines have just begun to provide flights on this route. What will be the likely result (or results) of this competition? *(Circle one or more answers.)*

a. elimination of consumer choice

b. lower prices for consumers

c. higher prices for consumers

d. increase in services offered to customers

e. fewer flights each day between the cities

A teenager has been given a gift of $500. She has wanted to save money to buy a car next year. Her savings bank is offering 6% interest on money. She has a CD player, but wishes she had a better one. A friend shows her his new CD player-stereo system. She'd really like to have one just like it. Then she sees a splashy magazine ad, telling about a sale on that exact system. She can get it this week for just $475.

20. What are the positive incentives for her to put the $500 in the savings bank?

_____

21. What are the negative incentives for this same action (incentives NOT to save)?

_____

22. Which is NOT true of the United States Federal Reserve System?

a. It serves as the government's bank.

b. It controls and regulates the amount of money in the banking system.

c. It has no relationship to the daily banking of the average citizen.

d. It buys and sells U.S. dollars on foreign exchange markets.

e. It supervises banking practices in the Unites States.

Name _____

27

Choose the correct economic term from this page to finish each statement correctly. Write the term in the blank.

resources

one-crop

corporation

subsistence

diversified

nationalized

earned

interest

unearned

investment

capital

currency

exempt

incentives

entrepreneur

non-profit

risk

23. An economy that is based on the production of many different kinds of products, rather than just one or a few, is a(n) _____ economy.

24. Most non-profit organizations are _____ from paying taxes.

25. Energy, trees, money, and human time are examples of economic_____ .

26. A(n) _____ is a business firm owned by stockholders with the right to buy, sell, and make contracts.

27. A risk of money to get something in return is a(n) _____ .

28. On a(n) _____ farm, a farmer grows what the family needs, and has no products left over to sell.

29. A(n) _____ starts a business and manages all the aspects of that company, including the risks.

30. Money received from investments like savings accounts, stocks, or bonds, is _____ income.

31. _____ is a fee charged for borrowing money.

32. _____ income is gained from doing a job.

33. Money used to start a business is called _____ .

Middle Grade Book of Social Studies Tests

Copyright ©2001 by Incentive Publications, Inc., Nashville, TN.

Choose the correct economic term from this page to finish each statement correctly.
Write the term in the blank.

34. During a(n) _____, a country prohibits the sale of
    certain products or services to another country.

35. A(n) _____ can result from a long period
    of recession.

36. _____ is the rivalry between people or businesses for
    resources or customers.

37. Products consumers wish to have (but that are not essential to
    life) are _____.

38. _____ is a general period of rising prices.

39. After the costs of production have been paid and the goods
    continue to make money, a company will gain a _____ .

40. During a _____, businesses don't sell as much,
    unemployment grows, and people generally spend less money.

41. A(n) _____ is someone who buys goods or services.

42. _____ are essential items needed to maintain life.

43. When consumers have a strong desire for a product, the product
    is in high _____.

44. A(n) _____ is someone who supplies goods
    or services.

45. Buying on _____ is buying now and paying later.

balance of trade

wants

needs

profit

competition

recession

depression

inflation

consumer

demand

producer

embargo

credit

expansion

welfare

bonds

Middle Grade Book of Social Studies Tests

World Geography Skills Checklists

World Geography Test # 1:

GEOGRAPHICAL FEATURES

Test Location: pages 33–37

Skill	*Test Items*
Discriminate between features of physical and cultural geography	1–16
Identify causes of seasons and the effects of the Earth's revolution	17–19
Locate and identify the world's continents	20, 23, 25, 28, 32, 33, 36
Locate and identify major bodies of water in the world	21, 22, 24–27, 29–31, 34, 35, 37
Identify and describe kinds of landforms or types of water forms	39–49
Locate specific landforms or water bodies within the different hemispheres and continents	50–52
Compare locations of world landforms and bodies of water	53–54
Recognize the features of different continents	55–56
Locate the continents in comparison to lines of latitude	57
Identify factors that influence climate	58–60
Describe and locate the world's major climate patterns and zones	61–70

World Geography Test # 2:

WORLD REGIONS

Test Location: pages 38–41

Skill	*Test Items*
Identify political make-up of the world's major geographical regions	1–8
Identify geographical features of the major world regions	9–17
Locate regions according to their latitude and longitude placement	18–26
Recognize geographic features of the Pacific Region	27
Recognize geographic features of the Middle East-North Africa Region	28
Recognize geographic features of the Sub-Saharan African Region	29, 33, 35
Recognize geographic features of the North American Region	30, 35
Recognize geographic features of the Latin American Region	31
Recognize geographic features of the Southeast Asian Region	32
Recognize geographic features of the Eastern European Region	33
Recognize geographic features of the Western European Region	34

Middle Grade Book of Social Studies Tests

World Geography Test # 3:

IMPORTANT PLACES & SPACES

Test Location: pages 42–47

Skill	*Test Items*
Locate the world's continents	1–7
Locate major bodies of water	1–3, 6
Compare locations of hemispheres and continents in relation to bodies of water and lines of latitude	1–3, 6–7
Identify locations of countries within hemispheres	1–3
Recognize locations of countries in Central and South America	8–15
Recognize location of countries in relation to the equator	16
Compare locations of countries in relation to other countries and to bodies of water	17–18
Recognize locations of countries in Africa, Europe, and Asia	19–32
Recognize locations of major world cities	33–52
Locate countries within world regions	53, 56
Locate cities within world regions	54, 55, 57
Identify provinces of Canada	58
Compare locations of countries to one another using directions	59–62
Identify country or continent locations of world features	63–70
Show understanding of some aspects of world population	35–37
Recognize characteristics and aspects of various world cultural regions	39–50

World Geography Test # 4:

UNITED STATES GEOGRAPHY

Test Location: pages 48–51

Skill	*Test Items*
Recognize features of different U.S. regions	1–5
Recognize the locations of states	6–17
Identify locations of important bodies of water in the U.S.	18–23
Identify state locations of major U.S. cities	24–26
Recognize state locations of geographic features	27–34
Recognize and locate major cities in relation to other cities and features	35–39
Compare locations of cities	35–40

Middle Grade Book of Social Studies Tests

World Geography Test # 5:

HUMAN GEOGRAPHY

Test Location: pages 52–55

Skill	*Test Items*
Identify human characteristics of places	1–35
Recognize features of governments in world regions	2
Identify different language families	3
Recognize reasons why people live differently in different places	4
Recognize some patterns of movement in human history	5–6, 30
Identify economic basis for different cultures	7
Recognize political influences on the lives of groups of people	8
Use a graph to interpret world population changes	9–13
Identify and locate some cultural landmarks of the world	14–23
Define terms related to human geography	24–35
Recognize characteristics of urban areas	24
Recognize political changes of a place	26, 28, 33
Identify ways the land and climate affect the lives of people	30, 31, 34
Recognize reasons for differences in standard of living	35

Middle Grade Book of Social Studies Tests

GEOGRAPHICAL FEATURES

Name _____

Possible Correct Answers: 70

Date _____

Your Correct Answers: _____

Each item on Spike's list is a factor that would describe the physical or cultural geography of a country or region. For each item, write P (for physical geography) or C (for cultural geography).

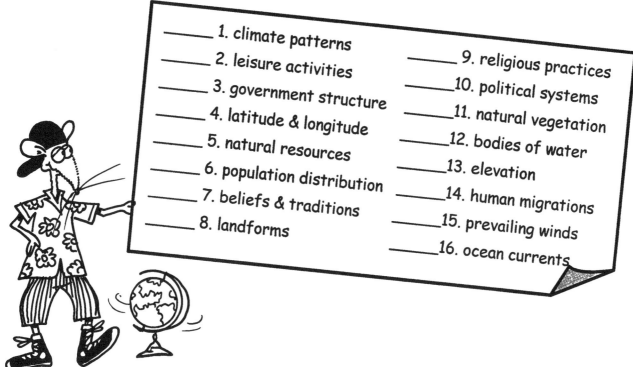

_____ 1. climate patterns

_____ 2. leisure activities

_____ 3. government structure

_____ 4. latitude & longitude

_____ 5. natural resources

_____ 6. population distribution

_____ 7. beliefs & traditions

_____ 8. landforms

_____ 9. religious practices

_____ 10. political systems

_____ 11. natural vegetation

_____ 12. bodies of water

_____ 13. elevation

_____ 14. human migrations

_____ 15. prevailing winds

_____ 16. ocean currents

Write a word or phrase to complete each sentence.

17. Seasons occur because of

the _____ of Earth.

18. During a vernal equinox in the southern hemisphere, the season beginning in the northern hemisphere is

_____ .

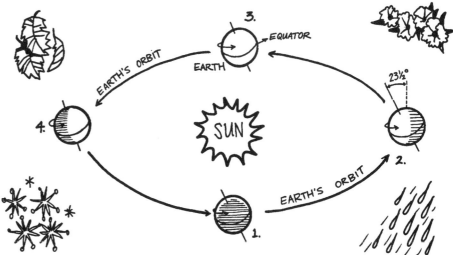

19. On the diagram, Earth would be in position # _____ during winter solstice in the northern hemisphere.

Write the correct letter from the world map to match the name of each continent or body of water listed below.

_____20. Australia

_____21. Pacific Ocean

_____22. South China Sea

_____23. Asia

_____24. Bering Sea

_____25. South America

_____26. Indian Ocean

_____27. Red Sea

_____28. Europe

_____29. North Sea

_____30. Atlantic Ocean

_____31. Mediterranean Sea

_____32. North America

_____33. Africa

_____34. Arctic Ocean

_____35. Hudson Bay

_____36. Antarctica

_____37. Caribbean Sea

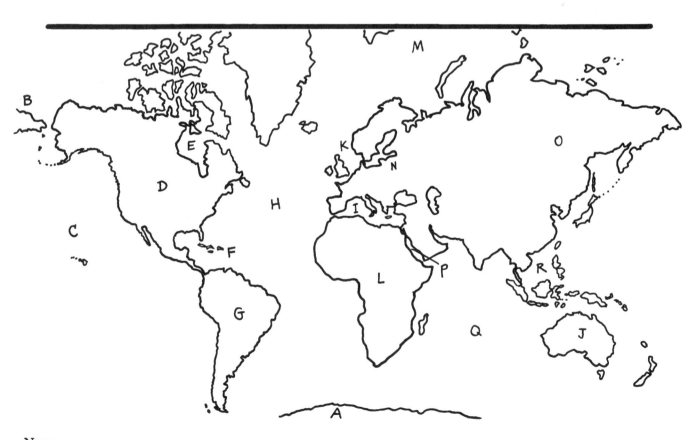

Where is Chester? Read each description.
Write the name of the landform or water body that describes his location.

butte   swamp

tundra   STEPPE

peninsula

continental shelf

GULF   isthmus

delta   glacier

mouth

archipelago

plain   seamount

SOURCE

cape   strait

plateau   canyon

CLIFF

_____ 38. Chester is standing on a piece of land that juts out into the sea, surrounded on three sides by water.

_____ 39. Chester is hiking near a spot in the mountains where a river begins.

_____ 40. Chester is kayaking between the islands in a chain of small islands.

_____ 41. Chester is snorkeling around an underwater mountain with steep sides.

_____ 42. Chester is digging for clams in a triangular-shaped area of land where a river deposits mud, sand, and rocks as it enters the sea.

_____ 43. Chester is sailing on a large area of sea that is partly surrounded by land.

_____ 44. Chester is fishing from a point of land that extends into the ocean.

_____ 45. Chester is exploring a large, thick bed of ice that is moving very slowly down a slope.

_____ 46. Chester is getting ready to hang glide from a high steep rock face.

_____ 47. Chester is climbing down the sides of a steep valley which was cut into the rock by a river.

_____ 48. Chester is cycling across a narrow strip of land that connects two larger bodies of land.

_____ 49. Chester is peering through a telescope on a large, level area of land that stands higher than the surrounding land.

Name _____

Middle Grade Book of Social Studies Tests

50. Which mountain ranges are found in the Eastern Hemisphere?

a. Rockies   e. Himalayas

b. Alps   f. Sierra Nevada

c. Andes   g. Urals

d. Pyrenees   h. Carpathians

51. Which of these are found in the Western Hemisphere?

a. Yucatan Peninsula

b. Alaskan Peninsula

c. Somali Peninsula

d. Baja Peninsula

e. Arabian Peninsula

52. Which features are found on the African continent?

a. Tigris River   f. Tibetan Plateau

b. Nile River   g. Congo Basin

c. Balkan Sea   h. Lake Victoria

d. Sahara Desert   i. Rift Valley

e. Siberian Plain   j. Kalahari Desert

53. Which of these lies farthest north?

a. West Siberian Plain

b. Mediterranean Sea

c. Persian Gulf

d. Lake Superior

e. Crater Lake

54. Which of these lies furthest south?

a. Cape of Good Hope

b. Cape Horn

c. Cape Cod

d. Indonesian Islands

e. Gulf of Mexico

55. Which continent contains these features? _____
(Strait of Gibraltar, Pyrenees Mountains, English Chanel, Black Sea, White Sea)

56. Which continent contains these features? _____
(Pampas, Andes Mountains, Lake Maracaibo, Cape Horn, Amazon River)

57. Which continents lie along the equator ?
(Include the islands associated with the continent.)

_____

58. In the middle latitudes (30°-60°), the prevailing winds are
    a. trade winds.   b. cyclonic storms.   c. westerlies.   d. easterlies.   e. polar winds.

59. The trade winds are most prevalent in the region of
    a. 60°–90° latitude.   b. the equator.   c. the poles.   d. the middle latitudes.

60. The factor below that does NOT contribute to controlling climate is
    a. elevation.   b. longitude.   c. ocean currents.   d. prevailing winds.
    e. topography.   f. elevation.   g. latitude.   h. land-water distribution.

How has Spike done on his true-false geography test? Circle the answers that are correct.

GEOGRAPHY TEST _____

Write T for true, and F for false.

__T__ 61. In a tropical savanna climate, there is usually a long, dry winter.

__F__ 62. In a Mediterranean climate, the summers are hot and dry, while the winters are mild.

__F__ 63. Forests are not found in humid continental climate areas.

__T__ 64. The Amazon Basin is a large area of tropical rainforest climate.

__F__ 65. A temperate marine climate would be found along the coast of northern California.

__F__ 66. In a semi-arid tropical climate, there is no precipitation at all.

__F__ 67. The Great Plains of the U.S. lie in a dry continental climate zone.

__F__ 68. In a true tropical desert area, it never rains.

__T__ 69. Low bushes and mosses grow in the area of Greenland that falls into a polar ice cap climate region.

__T__ 70. Polar tundra climate regions are found in the northern parts of North America, Europe, and Asia.

Middle Grade Book of Social Studies Tests

WORLD REGIONS

Name _____

Possible Correct Answers: 35

Date _____

Your Correct Answers: _____

The chart names nine geographical-cultural world regions. Refer to the chart as you answer these questions (1–8). Circle one or more answers for each question.

WORLD REGIONS

Western Europe
Eastern Europe & Russia
Eastern & Southern Asia
Middle East & North Africa
Sub-Saharan Africa
The Pacific *(Oceania)*
North America
Middle America *(Central America)*
South America

1. Which of the following countries would be found in the same region as Angola, Zambia, and Nigeria?
   a. Zaire   b. Botswana
   c. Algeria   d. Morocco

2. Which of the following countries, nations, or territories would be found in the same region as Samoa and Australia?
   a. Papua New Guinea   b. North Korea
   c. New Zealand   d. India
   e. Iran   f. Guam

3. Which of the following countries would be found in the same region as Luxembourg and Portugal?
   a. Spain   b. Georgia
   c. Denmark   d. Belgium
   e. Norway   f. Pakistan

4. Which of the following countries would be found in the same region as Argentina, Guyana, and Ecuador?
   a. Belize   b. Sierra Leone
   c. Peru   d. Colombia

5. Which of the following countries would be found in the same region as Russia, Albania, and Romania?
   a. Sweden   b. Belarus
   c. Hungary   d. Switzerland

6. Which of the following countries would be found in the same region as Thailand, China, and India?
   a. Vietnam   b. Yemen
   c. Japan   d. Philippines
   e. Oman   f. Laos

7. Which of the following countries would be found in the same region as Haiti, Guatemala, and Nicaragua?
   a. Honduras   b. Brazil
   c. Albania   d. Jamaica

8. Which of the following countries would be found in the same region as Egypt, Algeria, and Kuwait?
   a. Jordan   b. Uganda
   c. Iran   d. Syria

38

A traveler is considering visits to the different regions of the world. Read the geographic features of each region. Write the name of the region. Use the chart on page 1 of this test to find the region names.

9._____
- mostly south of the equator
- home to the Patagonia
- high mountains and rain forests
- home to Cape Horn
- home to the Amazon River

10._____
- thousands of islands
- home to smallest continent
- climate influenced by the ocean
- mostly south of the equator

11._____
- land of dry deserts
- major natural resource is oil
- borders the Mediterranean, Red, & Black Seas
- home to the Atlas Mountains
- home to the Nile River Delta

12._____
- holds world's largest country
- home to Siberian Plains
- home to the Ural Mountains
- north of the Tropic of Cancer
- borders the Arctic Ocean

13._____
- home to many islands
- connects two other regions
- home to the Yucatan Peninsula
- borders the Caribbean Sea
- home to the Isthmus of Panama

14._____
- north of the Tropic of Cancer
- home to the British Isles
- home to the Iberian & Italian Peninsulas
- home to the Alps Mountains
- borders the Mediterranean & North Seas

15._____
- borders Pacific & Indian Oceans
- home to many island countries
- home to world's highest mountains
- contains the Indian subcontinent
- home to the Mekong River

16._____
- home to the Mojave Desert
- borders the Arctic, Pacific, & Atlantic Oceans
- home to the Great Lakes & Hudson Bay
- home to Cascade & Appalachian Mountains
- home to the Amazon River

17._____
- land of rainforests and grasslands
- home to Lake Victoria
- home to the Kalahari Desert
- home to Cape of Good Hope

Name _____

Middle Grade Book of Social Studies Tests

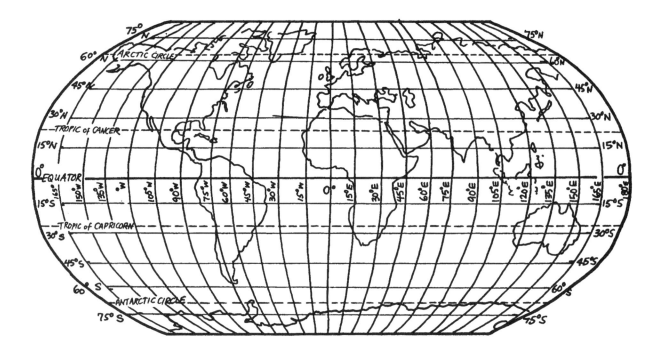

Locate these regions according to their latitude and longitude placement on Earth.

Write the letter code for each region next to the correct latitude-longitude description. (The latitude-longitude locations given here are approximate locations for the region.)

_____ 18. 25° N - 35° S latitude and 20° W - 50° E longitude

_____ 19. 90° N - 25° N latitude and 30° E - 170° E longitude

_____ 20. 80° N - 35° N latitude and 10° W - 30° E longitude

_____ 21. 20° N - 35° S latitude and 110° W - 180° W longitude

_____ 22. 80° N - 35° N latitude and 10° E - 170° W longitude

_____ 23. 10° N - 60° S latitude and 80° W - 35° W longitude

_____ 24. 50° N - 45° S latitude and 60° E - 180° E longitude

_____ 25. 45° N - 15° N latitude and 15° W - 65° E longitude

_____ 26. 30° N - 10° N latitude and 120° W - 60° W longitude

WORLD REGIONS

WE	Western Europe
EE	Eastern Europe & Russia
AS	Eastern & Southern Asia
ME	Middle East & North Africa
SSA	Sub-Saharan Africa
P	The Pacific (Oceania)
NA	North America
MA	Middle America (Central America)
SA	South America

Name _____

Middle Grade Book of Social Studies Tests

27. Which statement is not true of the Pacific Region?
    a. Most of the area is subject to earthquakes and tremors.
    b. Heavy rainfall is a feature of the climate in most of the region.
    c. Most of the countries are ruled by monarchies.

28. Which statement is not true of the Middle East-North Africa region?
    a. The religions of Judaism and Islam are about equal in the number of followers.
    b. The region has large reserves of petroleum.
    c. The region is the scene of division and strife between Arabs and Israelis

29. Which statement is true of the Sub-Saharan African Region?
    a. Until recently, many of the nations were held as colonies by European nations.
    b. The decolonization of the region has occurred without bloodshed.
    c. The nations are enjoying a fast rate of industrialization.

30. Which statements are true of both the United States and Canada?
    a. English is the only official language of the country.
    b. The country has a representative form of government.
    c. The people are a mixture of many cultural backgrounds.

31. Which statements are true of the Middle American and South American regions?
    a. Coffee, bananas, and sugarcane are major exports.
    b. The population is a blend of Indian, European, and African people.
    c. All of the nations today are governed by democratic systems.

32. The economy of Southeast Asia is
    a. primarily agriculture-based
    b. heavily industrialized
    c. mostly industrialized

33. Which regions of the world have experienced major changes in political structure in the twentieth century?
    a. North America   c. Western Europe
    b. Eastern Europe   d. Sub-Saharan Africa

34. Which region was the homeland of the following great writers, musicians, and artists: William Shakespeare, Charles Dickens, Leonardo da Vinci, Michelangelo, Henrik Ibsen, Wolfgang Mozart, Johann Sebastian Bach?
    a. Eastern Europe   c. Southeast Asia
    b. Western Europe   d. North America

35. Identify the areas of the world in which the economies would be called "developing economies" rather than "highly developed economies".
    a. Western Europe
    b. Sub-Saharan Africa
    c. Central America
    d. North America

Name

41

IMPORTANT PLACES & SPACES

Name _____   Possible Correct Answers: 70

Date _____   Your Correct Answers: _____

1. A sailor leaves the coast of Congo and sails straight west. He will cross the _____ (body of water) and eventually reach the country of _____.

2. A sailor sails directly south from the southern coast of Greece. He will cross the _____ (body of water) and reach the continent of _____.

3. A pilot is taking off from an airport in Nova Scotia, Canada. He will fly directly east, crossing the (body of water) _____ . The first continent he will reach is _____.

4. A world traveler explores the Southern Hemisphere. Which continents are NOT there for her to explore? _____

5. Another traveler explores the entire continent of Africa. Which hemispheres will she visit?

_____

6. Aristotle Rat visits a continent that borders the Atlantic Ocean, the Indian Ocean, the Arctic Ocean, the Red Sea, and the Mediterranean Sea. Where is he?

_____

7. Aristotle's friend, Spike, visits a continent that is all or partly below the Tropic of Capricorn. Which continent(s) could this be?

_____

_____

Name the country that matches each numbered location on the map.
Spelling will not count toward your score. Do your best to spell the country correctly.

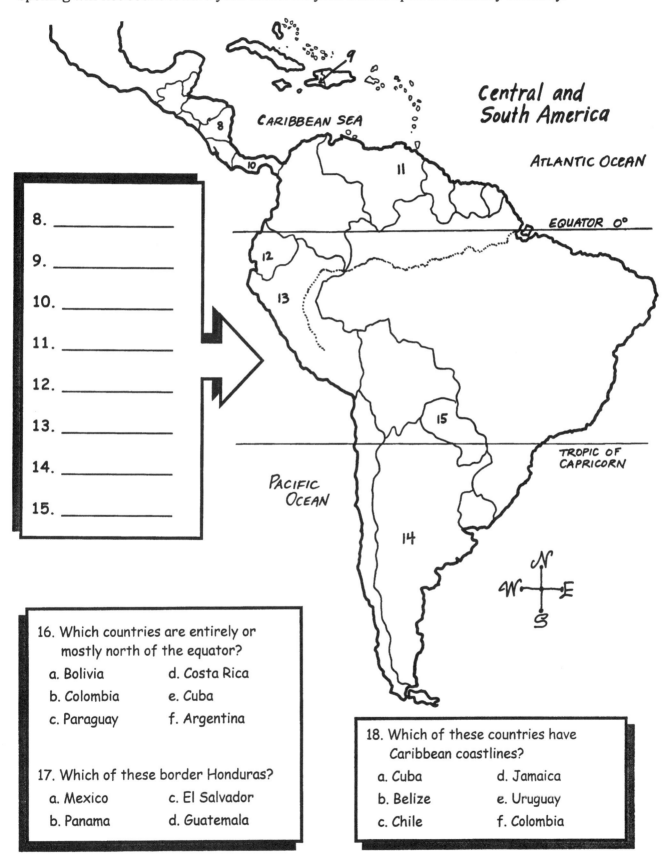

8. _____

9. _____

10. _____

11. _____

12. _____

13. _____

14. _____

15. _____

16. Which countries are entirely or
    mostly north of the equator?

   a. Bolivia   d. Costa Rica

   b. Colombia   e. Cuba

   c. Paraguay   f. Argentina

17. Which of these border Honduras?

   a. Mexico   c. El Salvador

   b. Panama   d. Guatemala

18. Which of these countries have
    Caribbean coastlines?

   a. Cuba   d. Jamaica

   b. Belize   e. Uruguay

   c. Chile   f. Colombia

Name _____

Middle Grade Book of Social Studies Tests

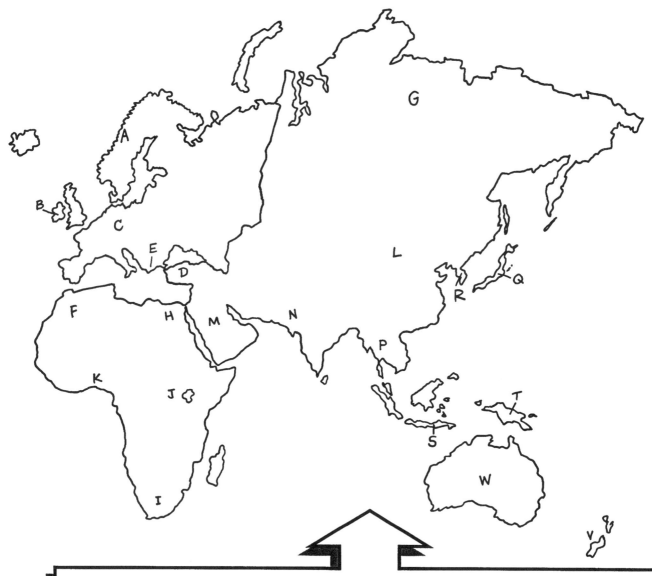

Write the letter that shows the approximate location of each country below.

_____ 19. Egypt

_____ 20. Saudi Arabia

_____ 21. Thailand

_____ 22. Germany

_____ 23. Turkey

_____ 24. Papua New Guinea

_____ 25. Algeria

_____ 26. Zaire

_____ 27. Norway

_____ 28. Indonesia

_____ 29. Russia

_____ 30. Pakistan

_____ 31. Nigeria

_____ 32. Greece

Name _____

This e-mail address book shows the names and cities of Aristotle's friends around the world. Write the country where each friend lives.

screen name	city	country	screen name	city	country
33. Singgy	Singapore		43. Pierre	Quebec	
34. Sammy	Seoul		44. Quizmo	Quito	
35. Surfer G.	Havana		45. B.J.	Bangkok	
36. Buddy B.	Bucharest		46. Dancer	Caracas	
37. Sparta	Rome		47. Buff	Berlin	
38. Benjy	Beijing		48. Diver	Acapulco	
39. Catya	Cairo		49. Rico	Rio de Janeiro	
40. Mozart	Vienna		50. Pricilla	Pretoria	
41. B. Biker	Sydney		51. Bobbo	Belfast	
42. Tamale	La Paz		52. Sukie	Stockholm	

Name _____

Middle Grade Book of Social Studies Tests

53. Which countries are in Southeast Asia?

| Laos | Burma | Cambodia | Pakistan |
| Afghanistan | Vietnam | Malaysia | Korea |

54. Which cities are NOT in Western Europe?

| Copenhagen | Sacramento | Damascus | Paris |
| Lisbon | Brussels | Florence | Helsinki |

55. Which city is NOT in North America?

| Winnipeg | Vancouver | Johannesburg | Baton Rouge |
| Anchorage | Quebec | Ottawa | Victoria |

56. Which country is NOT in Africa?

| Ethiopia | Ghana | Angola | Chad |
| Liberia | Sri Lanka | Mali | Sudan |

57. Which city is NOT in Central America or South America?

| Madrid | Montevideo | Concepción |
| Managua | San Jose | Bogotá |

58. Which of these is NOT a Canadian province?

| Alberta | Ontario | Nova Scotia |
| Manitoba | Greenland | British Colombia |

59. Which countries are WEST of Ukraine?

| Poland | Turkmenistan | Iran |
| Austria | Bangladesh | Netherlands |

60. Which countries are SOUTH of the Sahara Desert?

| Libya | Ghana | Congo, Kenya |
| Morocco | Zambia | Algeria Egypt |

61. Which country is CLOSEST to India?

| Iraq | Nepal | Turkey | South Korea |

62. Which country is CLOSEST to Hungary?

| Romania | Belgium | Finland | Spain |

Name

46

Where would you find . . .

63. Sardinia?
    a. in the Black Sea
    b. in the Mediterranean Sea
    c. in the North Sea
    d. in the Caspian Sea

64. the Strait of Gibraltar?
    a. between Saudi Arabia and Iran
    b. between France and England
    c. between Spain and Morocco
    d. between Malaysia and Indonesia

65. Mount Everest?
    a. in India
    b. in Iran
    c. In Tibet
    d. in Mongolia

66. the Great Barrier Reef?
    a. off the coast of Japan
    b. off the coast of Australia
    c. off the coast of Brazil
    d. off the coast of South Africa

67. On which continent would you find these? _____
    Appalachian Mountains   Great Salt Lake
    Great Plains   Rio Grande River

68. On which continent would you find these? _____
    Gobi Desert   Indus River
    Lake Baikal   Mekong Delta

69. On which continent would you find these? _____
    Victoria Falls   the Congo River   the Rift Valley

70. On which continent would you find these? _____
    The Pyrenees Mountains   Lapland   the Danube River

Name _____

Middle Grade Book of Social Studies Tests

UNITED STATES GEOGRAPHY

Name _____   Possible Correct Answers: 40

Date _____   Your Correct Answers: _____

1. Spike has just flown over Mt. St. Helens, Crater Lake, the Cascade Mountain Range, and a forest of the world's largest trees. Which region of the United States is he exploring?

    a. Plains Region

    b. Pacific Region

    c. New England Region

    d. Southwest Region

    e. Great Lakes Region

    f. Middle Atlantic Region

    g. Southeast Region

    h. Mountain Region

2. Next, he flies over the Potomac River, Niagara Falls, and the Hudson River. He's also been viewing some of the country's most heavily populated areas

    a. New England Region

    b. Southwestern Region

    c. Great Lakes Region

    d. Middle Atlantic Region

    e. Southeastern Region

3. Now, Spike is flying over the country's smallest state, looking down at fishing towns and rocky beaches. He's enjoying the beautiful fall colors of thousands of maple trees. Where is he?

    a. Pacific Region

    b. New England Region

    c. Southwestern Region

    d. Middle Atlantic Region

    e. Southeastern Region

4. He flies over North Dakota, Kansas, Iowa, and Nebraska. Which U.S. region is he enjoying?

    a. Plains Region Region

    b. Pacific Region

    c. New England Region

    d. Southwest Region

    e. Great Lakes Region

    f. Middle Atlantic Region

    g. Southeast Region

    h. Mountain Region

5. When he flies over the French Quarter of New Orleans, Stone Mountain, the Everglades, and Nashville's Grand Ole Opry, where is he?

    a. Plains Region

    b. Pacific Region

    c. New England Region

    d. Southwestern Region

    e. Great Lakes Region

    f. Middle Atlantic Region

    g. Southeastern Region

    h. Mountain Region

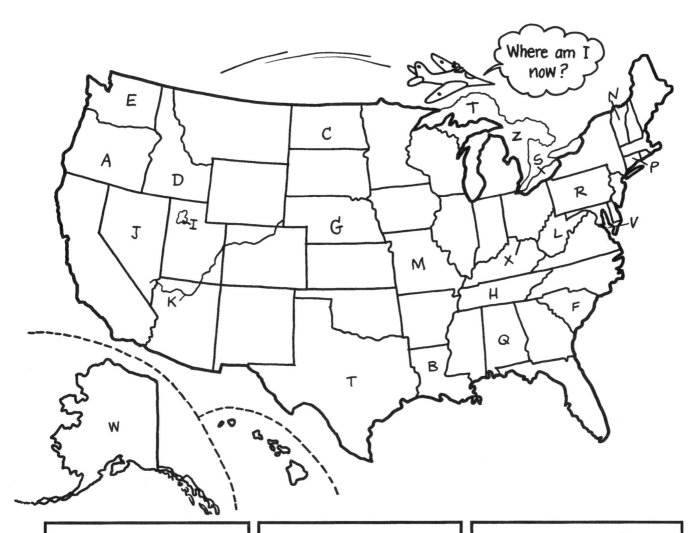

Where am I now?

Write the letter for each state.	
6. Nebraska	_____
7. Tennessee	_____
8. Missouri	_____
9. Alabama	_____
10. Oregon	_____
11. Nevada	_____

Write the letter for each state.	
12. South Carolina	_____
13. West Virginia	_____
14. Vermont	_____
15. Connecticut	_____
16. North Dakota	_____
17. Idaho	_____

Write the letter for each body of water.	
18. Great Salt Lake	_____
19. Lake Superior	_____
20. Colorado River	_____
21. Ohio River	_____
22. Chesapeake Bay	_____
23. Lake Erie	_____

24. Cities: Baton Rouge, New Orleans   The state:_____

25. Cities: Tacoma, Seattle, Spokane   The state:_____

26. Cities: Harrisburg, Scranton, Philadelphia   The state:_____

Name _____

49

27. Aristotle is vacationing near Mauna Loa. Where could he be?
    a. in Alaska   b. in Hawaii   c. in Washington   d. in Idaho

28. Aristotle is trying to climb Mt. McKinley. Where could he be?
    a. in Hawaii   b. in Alaska   c. in Colorado   d. in Wyoming

29. Aristotle is hiking in the Mojave Desert. Where could he be?
    a. in Oklahoma b. in Nevada   c. in California   d. in New Mexico

Where could I be ?

30. Aristotle is looking across the Rio Grande River. Where could he be?
    a. in Texas   b. in Arizona
    c. in Mississippi   d. in Oklahoma

31. Aristotle is taking a helicopter ride over the Grand Canyon. Where could he be?
    a. in New Mexico   b. in Texas
    c. in Arizona   d. in Nevada

32. Aristotle is taking pictures of alligators in the Everglades. Where could he be?
    a. in Florida   b. in Alabama
    c. in Louisiana   d. in Georgia

33. Aristotle is getting into his canoe on the shores of Lake Huron. Where could he be?
    a. in New York   b. in Michigan
    c. in Ohio   d. Wisconsin

34. Aristotle is just pushing a raft into the Mississippi River. Which state could he NOT be in?
    a. Illinois   b. North Dakota
    c. Arkansas   d. Tennessee

Name   **50**

35.
Who is in Chicago?
_____

Spike is in a city northeast of Indianapolis.
Gigi is on the shore of Lake Michigan.
Aristotle is in a city southwest of Des Moines.

36.
Who is in Albuquerque?
_____

Aristotle is on the border of Mexico.
Spike is in a city southwest of Denver.
Chichi is directly east of Salt Lake City.

37.
Who is in Little Rock?
_____

Spike is further south than Lexington.
Aristotle is further east than Atlanta.
Gigi is further north than Memphis.

38.
Who is in St. Louis?
_____

Aristotle is on the Mississippi River.
Spike is on the Ohio River.
Gigi is on the Colombia River.

39.
Who is in Buffalo?
_____

Aristotle is west of Boise.
Spike is just across the border
   from Ontario, Canada.
Gigi is on the Chesapeake Bay.

40. Which statements are true? *(Circle one or more.)*

A. Pittsburgh is farther west than Baltimore or Roanoke or Birmingham.

B. Pierre is northeast of Reno.

C. New Orleans is southwest of Chattanooga.

D. Baton Rouge is further east than Minneapolis, Detroit, or Wichita.

HUMAN GEOGRAPHY

Name _____   Possible Correct Answers: 35

Date _____   Your Correct Answers: _____

1. Which of these world areas has the least stable governments?
   a. Western Europe   b. North America
   c. the Middle East   d. East & Equatorial Africa

2. Which does NOT name one of the world's language families?
   a. Indo-European   b. North-South American
   c. Malayo-Polynesian   d. Sino-Tibetan   e. Uralic-Altaic

3. A reason why people build different kinds of houses is
   a. availability of building materials
   b. closeness to work or a way to make a living
   c. shelter and protection from a particular climate
   d. differing senses of beauty and design
   e. all of the above

4. In which of the following countries are more of the businesses and industries privately-operated (as opposed to run by the government)? (Choose one or more answers.)
   a. Hong Kong   b. China   c. North Korea   d. Japan   e. Germany

5. In the late twentieth century, the largest groups of immigrants to the U. S. have been
   a. Western & Eastern European.   b. Asian & Latin American.   c. African.

6. A group of immigrants to the United States who did not come willingly were the
   a. Eastern Europeans.   b. Western Europeans.   c. Africans.   d. Latin Americans.

7. An area of the world whose economy is largely based on farming and ranching, and which is the largest producer of wool for the world is
   a. Western Europe.   b. Russia.   c. New Zealand.   d. Brazil.

8. The policy of apartheid in South Africa formed categories of citizens based on
   a. religion.   b. race.   c. economic status.   d. population distribution.

Middle Grade Book of Social Studies Tests   Copyright ©2001 by Incentive Publications, Inc., Nashville, TN.

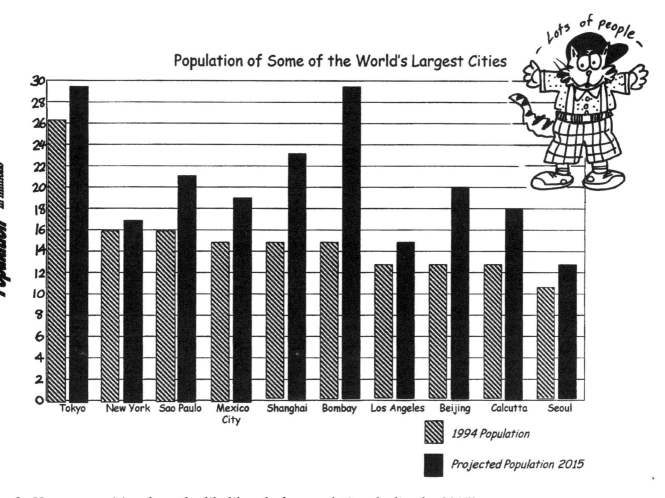

Population of Some of the World's Largest Cities

9. How many cities show the likelihood of a population decline by 2015?

_____

10. How many cities are likely to have a population over 20 million by 2015?

_____

11. How many cities have a greater population in 2015 than New York had in 1994?

_____

12. Which city is likely to have the greatest growth between 1994 and 2015?

_____

13. Which city is likely to have the least growth between 1994 and 2015?

_____

Name _____

Middle Grade Book of Social Studies Tests

A visitor is describing one of the great cultural landmarks of the world.
Write the name of the country in which the landmark would be found.

I was welcomed to a harbor by a huge lady, the Statue of Liberty, who was a gift from France.

14._____

They don't ring the bells any longer here at the Leaning Tower of Pisa.

15._____

I've just walked across the Thames River on the famous London Bridge.

16._____

I have not yet walked the whole length of this 1500-mile wall, but I learned that it is the only man-made structure on Earth that can be seen from the moon.

17._____

I've enjoyed a view of the whole city from the Eiffel Tower.

18._____

The ancient monument of Stonehenge was probably built back in the Stone Ages.

19._____

I've just enjoyed a ride through this 51-mile long canal that connects the Atlantic and Pacific Oceans.

20._____

The ancient pyramids at Giza are huge. One covers 13 acres!

21._____

The magnificent Taj Mahal is actually a tomb built by a Shah for his young wife.

22._____

The Colosseum is partly in ruins now, but it once held splendid sporting events.

23._____

Name _____

54

Write the correct term to complete each sentence.

24. A(n) _____ is someone who studies cultures.

25. The city of Los Angeles and its many suburbs are all crowded so close together that they form one huge, continuous city area, called a(n) _____.

26. Australia is a member of the _____, a group of nations once ruled by Great Britain.

27. A study of _____ involves learning about the population distribution and changes of an area.

28. In Africa, many countries have fought hard for _____

(the right to self-government).

29. A(n) _____ group shares a language, history, or place of origin.

30. The Bedouin people of North Africa are _____, moving from place to place to find food and water for their animals.

United Nations

demographics

nomads

arable

megalopolis

geologist

standard of living

autonomy

government

suburb

population density

anthropologist

irrigation

Commonwealth

separatists

cost of living

ethnic

31. Some countries suffer from a lack of _____ land

(land suitable for farming.)

32. _____ is found by dividing the area of a region by the number of people who live there.

33. In Canada, French _____ consider breaking away from the government in order to preserve their culture.

34. Throughout the world, _____ has allowed people to make a living on land that was once too dry for human use.

35. Western European countries enjoy a high _____ because of a high amount of goods and services available to the people.

Middle Grade Book of Social Studies Tests

Map Skills Checklists

Map Skills Test # 1:

MAP TOOLS & RESOURCES

Test Location: pages 58–61

Skill	Test Items
Distinguish between different kinds of maps	1–2
Understand and use the concept of scale on a map	3–4, 11–14
Identify parts of a map and their purposes	5–7
Read and use a map key	8–9
Understand the use of symbols on a map	8–9
Choose the best title for a map	10
Identify the world hemispheres	15–18
Recognize the major lines of latitude and the poles	19–25
Use a grid to locate features on a map	26–30
Place features on a grid map	31–35

Map Skills Test # 2:

DIRECTIONS, DISTANCES, & LOCATIONS

Test Location: pages 62–65

Skill	Test Items
Use scale to determine distances on maps	1–5
Find directions on maps	6–24
Identify and compare world locations	6–14
Find locations using lines of latitude and longitude	15–30
Identify and locate countries and cities in Europe	6–13
Identify and locate cities in Europe, Asia, Africa, and Australia	15–24
Use latitude and longitude to locate countries in Africa	25–30

Map Skills Test # 3:

FINDING INFORMATION ON MAPS

Test Location: pages 66–71

Skill	*Test Items*
Find information on a road map	1–4
Find information on a political map	5–8
Find information on an elevation map	9–13
Find information on a population map	14–19
Use a time zone map to find information and solve problems	20–24
Find information on a weather map	25–30

Middle Grade Book of Social Studies Tests

MAP TOOLS & RESOURCES

Name _____   Possible Correct Answers: 35

Date _____   Your Correct Answers: _____

1. Spike is headed for a safari in Eastern Africa. If he wants to find out the locations of cities and countries in the area, he should look at

    a. a road map.   b. a political map.

    c. a topographical map.   d. a product map.

2. On his trip, he is hoping to hike highlands and lowlands of the area. To find out the elevations and locations of valleys, plateaus, and mountains, he should look at

    a. a weather map.   b. a political map.

    c. a road map.   d. a topographical map.

3. Two cities on a map are 7 inches apart. The map's scale is 2 inches = 30 miles.

    How far apart are the cities? _____

4. A campsite on Lost Lake is 12 miles from the base of the Fire Lookout Tower. On a map of the area, the two locations are 4 cm. apart. What is the map's scale?

    a. 1 cm = 3 mi   b. 1 cm = 2 mic.

    c. 3 cm = 10 mi   d. 2 cm = 4 mi

Write a map part to answer each question.

_____5. Which gives information about distances?

_____6. Which shows the subject of the map?

_____7. Which explains the meaning of the symbols used?

Parts of a Map
title
scale
key
labels
symbols
compass rose

58

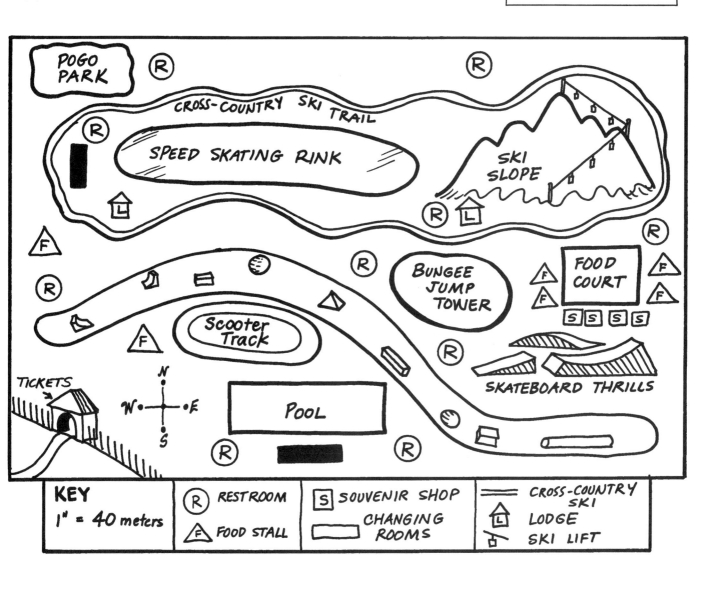

KEY
1" = 40 meters

ⓇRESTROOM
⚠ FOOD STALL
Ⓢ SOUVENIR SHOP
CHANGING ROOMS
═══ CROSS-COUNTRY SKI
⌂L LODGE
⚐ SKI LIFT

(11–15) Write T for True or F for False.

8. How many souvenir shops are found in the park? _____

9. How many restrooms are west of the Skate Board Thrills area? _____

10. What is the best title for the map?
    a. The Speed Skating Rink
    b. Sports County Road Map
    c. Sports Spectacular Theme Park
    d. The Pogo Park Area

_____11. The ski lift is about 70 meters long.

_____12. It is about 80 meters from the Entrance to the Pogo Park.

_____13. The distance around the Scooter Track is less than 100 meters.

_____14. A swimmer who did 20 length-wise laps (back & forth) in the pool covered about 2800 meters.

Name _____

Middle Grade Book of Social Studies Tests

Label each hemisphere: Eastern, Western, Northern, or Southern.

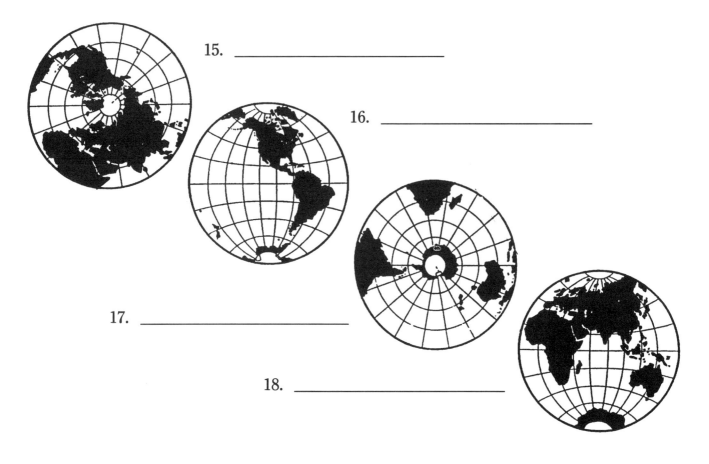

15. _____

16. _____

17. _____

18. _____

Name each major latitude location. Write the location in degrees, also. *(Example: 20° N Latitude.)*

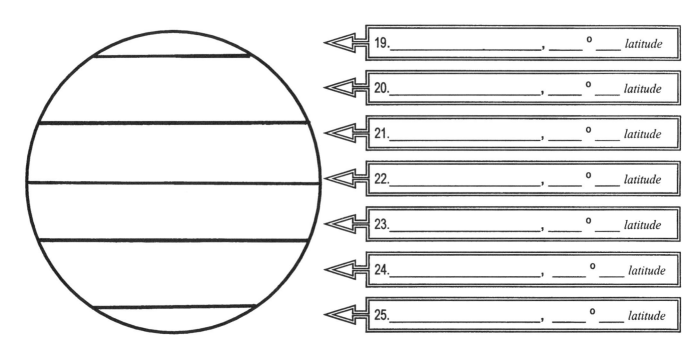

19. _____, ____ ° ____ latitude

20. _____, ____ ° ____ latitude

21. _____, ____ ° ____ latitude

22. _____, ____ ° ____ latitude

23. _____, ____ ° ____ latitude

24. _____, ____ ° ____ latitude

25. _____, ____ ° ____ latitude

Name _____

60

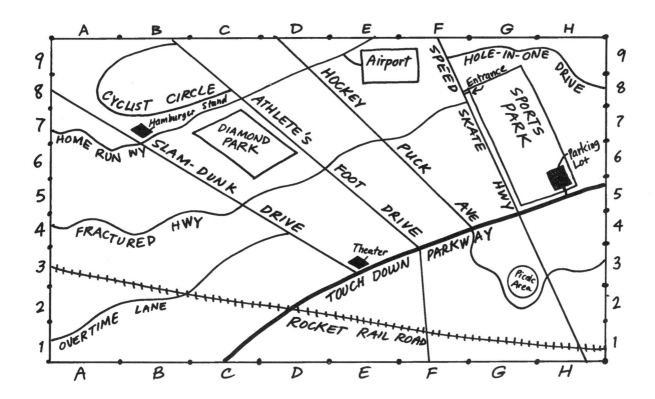

Circle the correct answer for 26-30.

26. Which is the approximate location of an entrance to the Sports Park?

    a. H4   b. G9   c. H4   d. F8

27. Overtime Lane intersects the railroad at which location?

    a. B2   b. F1   c. D2   d. C3

28. Where would you find Cyclist Circle?

    a. E7   b. H4   c. E4   d. B8

29. Which location would NOT be helpful in locating Athlete's Foot Drive?

    a. C9   b. E6   c. G7   d. F2

30. Jojo lives at C6. Which address is his?

    a. 1220 Speed Skate Highway
    b. 143 Hole-in-One Drive
    c. 1700 Slam-Dunk Drive
    d. 9 Cyclist Circle

Use a letter-number combination to show the approximate location for each:

_____ 31. Sports Park Parking Lot

_____ 32. Theater

_____ 33. Airport

_____ 34. Picnic Area

_____ 35. Hamburger Stand

Name _____

Middle Grade Book of Social Studies Tests

DIRECTIONS, DISTANCES, & LOCATIONS

Name _____

Date _____

Possible Correct Answers: 30

Your Correct Answers: _____

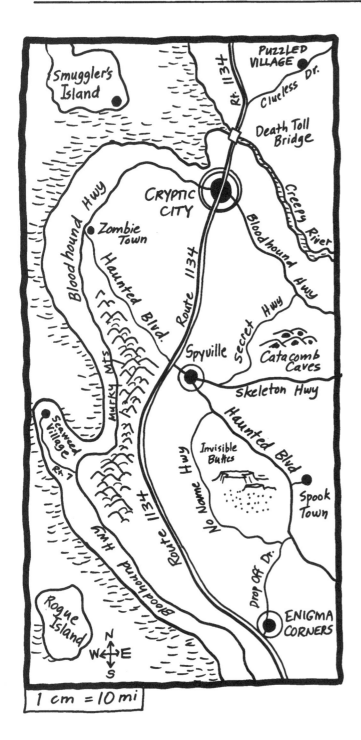

1 cm = 10 mi

1. The distance from Spyville to Enigma Corners on Route 1134 is about
   a. 9 miles   c. 120 miles
   b. 70 miles   d. 90 miles

2. What can be found about 130 miles southwest of Death Toll Bridge *(as an airplane flies)*?

   _____

3. What can be found about 35 miles northwest of Cryptic City?

   _____

4. Which of these is about 60 miles southeast of Seaweed Village?
   a. Rogue Island   d. Enigma Corners
   b. Spyville   e. Haunted Blvd.
   c. Invisible Buttes   f. Drop Off Dr.

5. About how far are the Catacomb Caves from Creepy River?
   a. about 200   c. about 2
   b. about 20   d. about 40

CITIES OF EUROPE

Write a direction in each blank:
N, S, E, W, NE, SE, NW, or SW.

6. Warsaw is _____ of Madrid.

7. Sofia is _____ of Bern.

8. Rome is _____ of Hamburg.

9. Moscow is _____ of Dublin.

10. Kiev is _____ of Paris.

11. Oslo is _____ of Dublin.

12. Spike visits a city that is not SW of the North Sea. Which city could it be?
a. Berlin   c. Budapest
b. Bucharest   d. Lisbon

13. He travels to a city that is NE of the Bay of Biscay. Which city could it be?
a. Naples   c. Istanbul
b. St. Petersburg d. Athens

14. Spike heads for a beach that is E of Sarajevo. Where is the beach?
a. Mediterranean Sea
b. Baltic Sea
c. Black Sea

Name _____

Middle Grade Book of Social Studies Tests

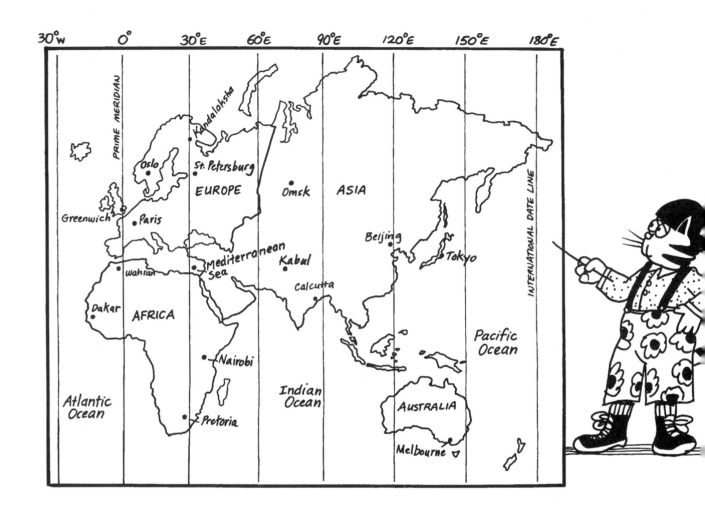

_____ 15. a city about 60° W of the International Date Line

_____ 16. a body of water between 0° and 40° E longitude

_____ 17. a city about at about 15° W longitude

_____ 18. a city about 140° east of Melbourne

_____ 19. a city lying at about 45° E longitude

_____ 20. a city about 15° east of Wahran

_____ 21. a body of water between 40° and 120° E longitude

_____ 22. a city about 20° east of Beijing

_____ 23. a city at 0° longitude

_____ 24. a city lying at about 35° E latitude

Name _____

Middle Grade Book of Social Studies Tests

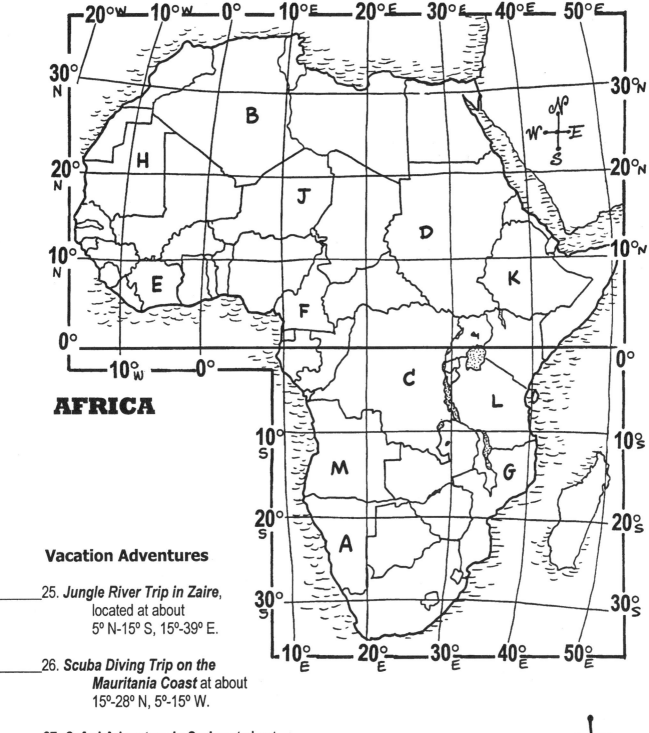

AFRICA

Vacation Adventures

_____ 25. *Jungle River Trip in Zaire*,
located at about
5º N-15º S, 15º-39º E.

_____ 26. *Scuba Diving Trip on the
Mauritania Coast* at about
15º-28º N, 5º-15º W.

_____ 27. *Safari Adventure in Sudan* at about
5º-23º N, 23º-38º E.

_____ 28. *Mountain Trek in Algeria* at about 20º-38º N, 8º W- 11º E.

_____ 29. *Beach Excursion in Mozambique* at about 20º-38º N, 8º W- 11º E.

_____ 30. *Diamond Mine Walk in Angola*, located at about 5º-18º S, 12º- 24º E.

Name _____

65

Middle Grade Book of Social Studies Tests

FINDING INFORMATION ON MAPS

Name _____   Possible Correct Answers: 30

Date _____   Your Correct Answers: _____

1. Which roads or highways cross the Oregon Trail? _____

   _____

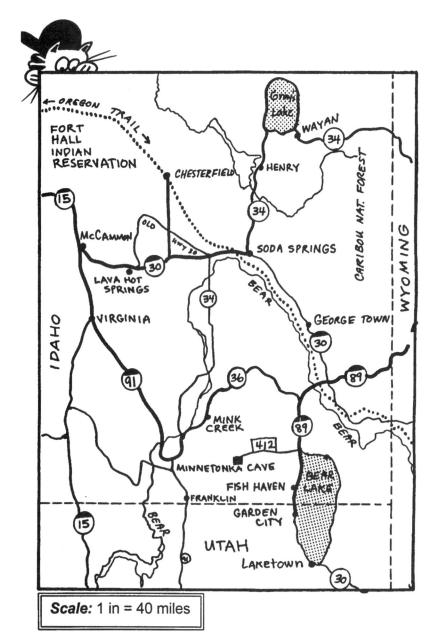

2. Which of these cities are in Idaho?
   a. Mink Creek
   b. Garden City
   c. Georgetown
   d. McCammon

3. About how far is it from Laketown to Soda Springs? (by airplane)
   a. 35 mi
   b. 70 mi
   c. 140 mi
   d. 1400 mi

4. About how far is Henry from the Wyoming border?
   a. 150 mi
   b. 60 mi
   c. 40 mi
   d. 80 mi

Scale: 1 in = 40 miles

66

CANADA

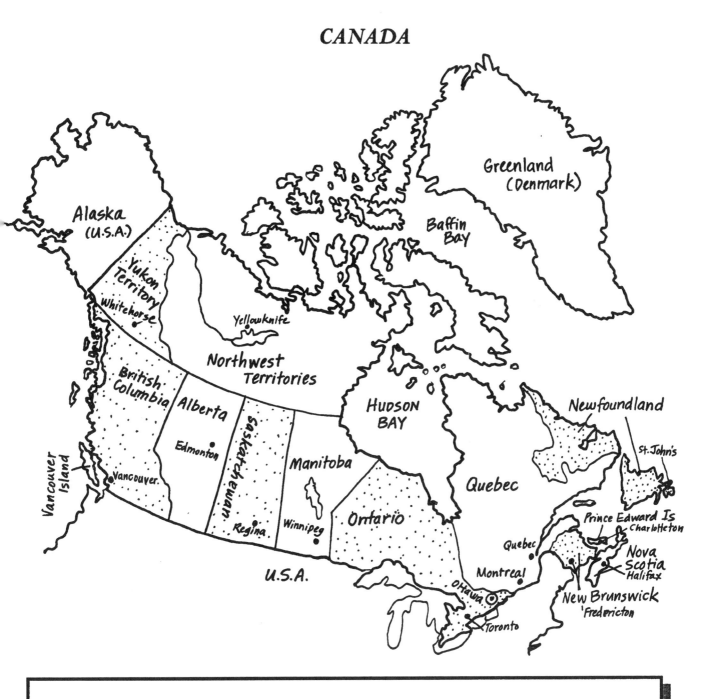

5. Which Canadian province is bordered by all five Great Lakes?_____

6. What provinces are islands?_____

7. What is the capital of British Columbia?_____

8. How many provinces border Hudson Bay?_____

Name _____ **67** _____

Middle Grade Book of Social Studies Tests

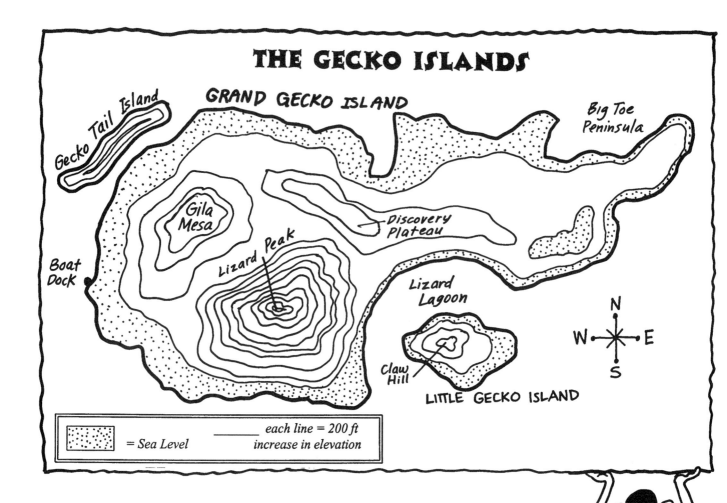

THE GECKO ISLANDS

Gecko Tail Island

GRAND GECKO ISLAND

Big Toe Peninsula

Gila Mesa

Discovery Plateau

Lizard Peak

Boat Dock

Lizard Lagoon

Claw Hill

LITTLE GECKO ISLAND

N
W   E
S

= Sea Level   _____ each line = 200 ft
               increase in elevation

9. Aristotle hikes from the boat dock up Gila Mesa.
   Then he hikes down the mesa back to the boat dock.
   How many feet (in elevation) does he cover in his hike?

   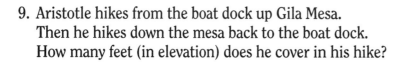

10. What is the elevation of Lizard Peak? _____

11. How much higher is Gila Mesa than Discovery Plateau?_____

12. What is the elevation of the highest point on Little Gecko Island?_____

13. What is the elevation of the highest point on Gecko Tail Island? _____

14. What is the gecko population of Lizard Peak Area?

_____

15. What is the gecko population of Jungle Valley?

_____

16. What is the difference between the population of the Desert Area and Gecko Tail Island?

_____

17. Which area has about 425 fewer geckos than Jungle Valley?

_____

18. What is the gecko population of the Desert Area?

_____

19. What is the difference between the population in the Gila Mesa Area and the Flood Plain Area?

_____

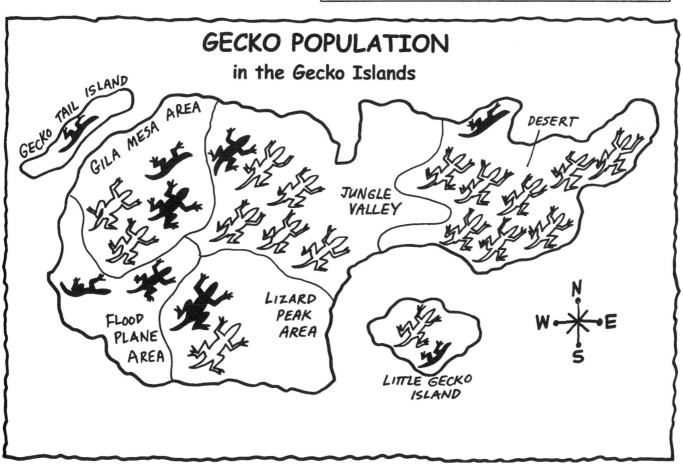

GECKO POPULATION
in the Gecko Islands

Name _____

69

Timely Delivery Express Company

WORLD TIME ZONES

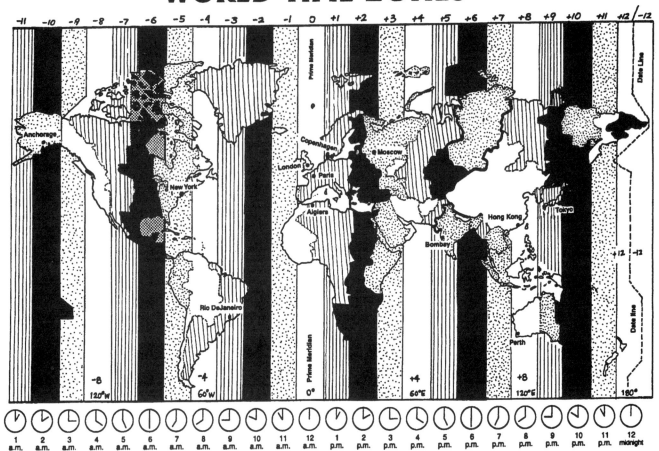

20. It is midnight in London. What time was it 5 hours ago in California? _____

21. It is noon in Rio De Janeiro. What time is it in Perth? _____

22. It is 4:30 P.M. in Hong Kong. What time is it in Copenhagen?_____

23. A 3½ -hour flight leaves Algiers at 8:40 A.M. What time will it arrive in Moscow?

    (Moscow time) _____

24. Spike flies east from Anchorage to Paris. His flight left Anchorage at 11:15 A.M. on Monday.
    He arrived in Paris at 2:15 P.M. on Tuesday. How long was his travel time?
    a. 27 hours
    b. 15 hours
    c. 17 hours
    d. 37 hours

Annual Rainfall in Mexico

Annual Rainfall in Mexico

 under 10"

 10" – 20"

 20" – 40"

 over 40"

25. The average rainfall in Chihuahua is _____.

26. The average yearly rainfall in Acapulco is_____.

27. La Paz gets about _____ fewer inches of rain a year than Acapulco.

28. Which cities get at least 15 inches more a year than Mexico City?_____

29. How many cities shown get less rainfall than Vera Cruz or Tampico?_____

30. Which city would be the best choice
for a sunny beach vacation any time of year?

_____

Name

Middle Grade Book of Social Studies Tests

World History Skills Checklists

World History Test # 1:
MAJOR ERAS & EVENTS IN WORLD HISTORY

Test Location: pages 75–81

Skill	Test Items
Distinguish between major conflicts in world history	1–8
Recognize major events in world history	9–18
Describe the significance of major events in world history	9–18
Recognize time period of major events in world history	20, 24
Recognize location of major events in world history	19, 21–23, 25–28
Recognize general chronology of events in world history	29–40
Recognize events that occurred in a similar time period	41–42
Place major eras on a timeline	43–50
Define terms related to world history	51–58
Describe changes caused by events in world history	59–60

World History Test # 2:
PEOPLE, PLACES, & ORGANIZATIONS IN WORLD HISTORY

Test Location: pages 82–87

Skill	Test Items
Identify key persons in world history	1–28
Identify key persons in ancient history; associate them with events, movements, or eras	2, 9
Identify key persons in world history 1000–2000; associate them with events, movements, or eras	1, 8, 10, 12, 14, 19, 20, 22, 24, 27
Identify key persons in 20th century; associate them with events, movements, or eras	2, 3–7, 11, 13, 15–18, 21, 25, 26
Identify and locate key places in world history	29–42
Associate world locations with events in history	29–50
Identify key features or purposes of world organizations	51–58
Identify purposes of agreements and institutions	59–65

World History Test # 3:

ANCIENT WORLD HISTORY

Test Location: pages 88–93

Skill	*Test Items*
Identify major events in ancient world history	1, 2
Identify major eras in ancient world history	2–7
Place events in the era in which they occurred	2–7
Identify key people in ancient world history	8–13
Identify locations of ancient civilizations	14–22
Recognize features of ancient Egyptian civilization	23, 24, 36
Recognize features of ancient Mesopotamia civilizations	25–30
Recognize features of ancient civilizations of the Indus River Valley	31, 33
Recognize features of ancient Chinese civilizations	32
Recognize features of ancient Greek civilization	34
Recognize features of ancient Roman civilization	35
Recognize features of ancient Latin American civilizations	36–38
Recognize and compare chronology of events in ancient world history	39–40

World History Test # 4:

MEDIEVAL & MODERN WORLD HISTORY THROUGH 1900

Test Location: pages 94–99

Skill	*Test Items*
Recognize key features and events of the Middle Ages	1, 5–7, 9, 10
Define and describe feudalism	2
Recognize features, events, and significance of the Renaissance	3
Define imperialism and colonization, and recognize the effects	8, 23–26
Recognize features, events, and significance of the Reformation	8, 20
Identify key events in the period from 1000–1900	1–10
Compare chronology of events in the period; place events on a timeline	11–19
Recognize features, events, and significance of the Industrial Revolution	21, 22
Identify the areas of the world colonized by European countries	23–26
Identify key persons in this period of world history; connect them with events or accomplishments	27–39
Recognize significant events during this period in Europe	1–26
Recognize significant events during this period in Africa	40–45
Recognize significant events during this period in Asia	46–48
Recognize significant events during this period in Latin America	49
Recognize significant events during this period in North America	50

Middle Grade Book of Social Studies Tests

World History Test # 5:

MODERN WORLD HISTORY SINCE 1900

Test Location: pages 100–105

Skill	*Test Items*
Identify and describe key events in modern world history since 1900	1–12, 13–32, 37–41
Describe the significance of selected events in history since 1900	1–12
Distinguish between major conflicts in world history since 1900	15–19
Identify causes of major conflicts in world history since 1900	15–19
Recognize purpose of major agreements in world history since 1900	20–27
Identify causes and results of World War 1	28–29
Identify causes and results of World War II	30–31
Recognize features of the Cold War period	32
Recognize features and purposes of organizations, plans, and policies in world history since 1900	33–36
Identify key developments and events in Europe since 1900	33–37, 42
Identify key developments and events in Latin America since 1900	38
Identify key developments and events in the Middle East since 1900	39
Identify key developments and events in Africa since 1900	40
Identify key developments and events in Asia since 1900	41
Recognize time period of events in world history since 1900	43–55
Place events on a timeline	43–52
Compare chronology of events in world history since 1900	53–55

Middle Grade Book of Social Studies Tests

MAJOR ERAS & EVENTS IN WORLD HISTORY

Name _____   Possible Correct Answers: 60

Date _____   Your Correct Answers: _____

Aristotle is wondering about all these conflicts in world history.
He's matching up the wars with their descriptions.
Has he got them straight? Circle the number of every one that he has
identified correctly. Write the CORRECT letter for any that he has wrong.

Conflicts in World History

A. Boer War

B. Opium Wars

C. Punic Wars

D. Persian Gulf War

E. 6-Day War

F. Vietnam War

G. 100 Years War

H. Mexican Revolution

I. American Revolution

J. Cold War

K. War of 1812

L. Korean War

M. Spanish-American War

N. War in Bosnia

O. Russian Revolution

P. French Revolution

Which War?

_____ 1. War between Israelis and Arabs over land in the Middle East

_____ 2. War in which U.S. sent troops in 1965 to help stop the possible spread of communist control throughout the whole country

_____ 3. Civil war between ethnic groups in areas that were a part of Yugoslavia before its 1992 break-up

_____ 4. War between England and France over who would have the greatest power in Europe

_____ 5. War sparked by settlers in South Africa who wanted to get rid of British control

_____ 6. War that began in 1950 in which U.N. troops joined to help stop the spread of communist control from a neighbor to the north

_____ 7. War between China and England over trade issues, including trade of an illegal drug

_____ 8. War in which U.S. attacked Iraq after Iraq invaded Kuwait over an oil dispute

75

Each headline refers to a major event in world history.
Below the headline, write the name or a brief description of the event,
or tell the importance of the event.

9. _____

Change in Europe Ends Dark Ages

10. _____

Archduke Ferdinand Assassinated

11. _____

SARAJEVO IN RUINS

12. _____

Greece Plans Games to Honor Zeus

13. _____

Treaty Signed at Yalta

14. _____

TWO BOMBS CHANGE THE WORLD

15. _____

New Nation Born in Middle East

16. _____

Communist Power Breaks Apart

17. _____

CURTAIN DIVIDES EUROPE

18. _____

Sputnik Ushers in a New Era

Each headline below refers to an event in world history.
Choose one answer that tells where or when the event occurred.

19.

Troops Storm Normandy

WHERE?
a. Australia   c. England
b. Italy   d. France

20.

THE ROMAN EMPIRE FALLS

WHEN?
a. 500 B.C.   c. 1540 A.D.
b. 476 A.D.   d. 1100 B.C.

21.

British Control Spreads Across Continent

WHERE?
a. Europe   c. Antarctica
b. Africa   d. South America

22.

GREAT WALL IS FINISHED

WHERE?
a. China   c. India
b. Russia   d. Japan

23.

Angry Settlers Take a Great Trek

WHERE?
a. Europe   c. Southern Africa
b. North Africa   d. South America

24.

PRIEST NAILS LIST TO DOOR

WHEN?
a. 800 B.C.   c. 1776 A.D.
b. 1517 A.D.   d. 1915 A.D.

25.

Indus River Valley Civilization Disappears

WHERE?
a. Central America   c. Africa
b. North America   d. India

26.

BAY OF PIGS INVASION FAILS

WHERE?
a. Hong Kong   c. Ecuador
b. Cuba   d. Russia

27.

Red Guard Enforces Cultural Revolution

WHERE?
a. Pakistan   c. Iran
b. Russia   d. China

28.

Fatal Shots in Tianamen Square

WHERE?
a. Bosnia   c. Brazil
b. China   d. Canada

Name

Middle Grade Book of Social Studies Tests

Circle one answer for each question.

Engarde!

29. Which happened **first**?
a. the Industrial Revolution
b. the Crusades
c .the Cold War
d. the Persian Gulf War

33. Who lived **first**?
a. Leonardo da Vinci
b. Salvadore Allende
c. Muhammad
d. Socrates

30. Which was written **first**?
a. Hammurabi's Code of Laws
b. the Magna Carta
c. the U.S. Constitution
d. the Napoleonic Code

34. Which happened **second**?
a. the end of World War II
b. the break-up of Soviet Union
c. the storming of Bastille
d. the Persian Gulf War

31. Which happened **first**?
a .the French Revolution
b. World War I
c. the Russian Revolution
d. the American Revolution

35. Which happened **second**?
a. the atomic bomb on Hiroshima
b. the Chinese Cultural Revolution
c. Soviet missiles in Cuba
d. the division of Czechoslovakia

32. Which happened **first**?
a. the founding of Israel
b. the Hebrew exodus from Egypt
c. the Camp David Peace Accord
d. the Six-Day War

36. Which happened **second**?
a. Copernicus confirmed that Earth is not the center of the universe.
b. Napoleon created a French empire.
c. The Soviet Union instituted the policy of glasnost.
d. Alexander the Great ruled all of Greece.

Name

Middle Grade Book of Social Studies Tests

37. Which happened **last**?
   a. the launch of Sputnik
   b. the invention of the steam engine
   c. the beginnings of the Internet
   d. Newton's Laws of Gravity

38. Which came **last**?
   a. British Empire   b. Ice Age   c. Mayan civilization   d. Egyptian Empire

39. Which came **last**?
   a. Vietnam War   b. First moon landing   c. The Holocaust   d. Rabin assassination

40. Who ruled **most recently**?
   a. Golda Meir   b. Josef Stalin   c. Charlemagne   d. Nelson Mandela

41. Which two events happened **about** the same time? (Circle two answers.)
   a. The New Stone Age began.
   b. Rome conquered Greece.
   c. The Old Babylonian Empire was at its peak.
   d. The Shang Dynasty began in China.

42. Which two events happened **about** the same time? (Circle two answers.)
   a. Feudalism spread across Europe.
   b. The policy of Apartheid was established in South Africa.
   c. The nation of Israel was founded.
   d. The English Bill of Rights created a new constitutional monarchy.

Name _____

Middle Grade Book of Social Studies Tests

Each letter from the timeline represents an event that took place in that general time period in world history. Write the correct letter next to each event below.

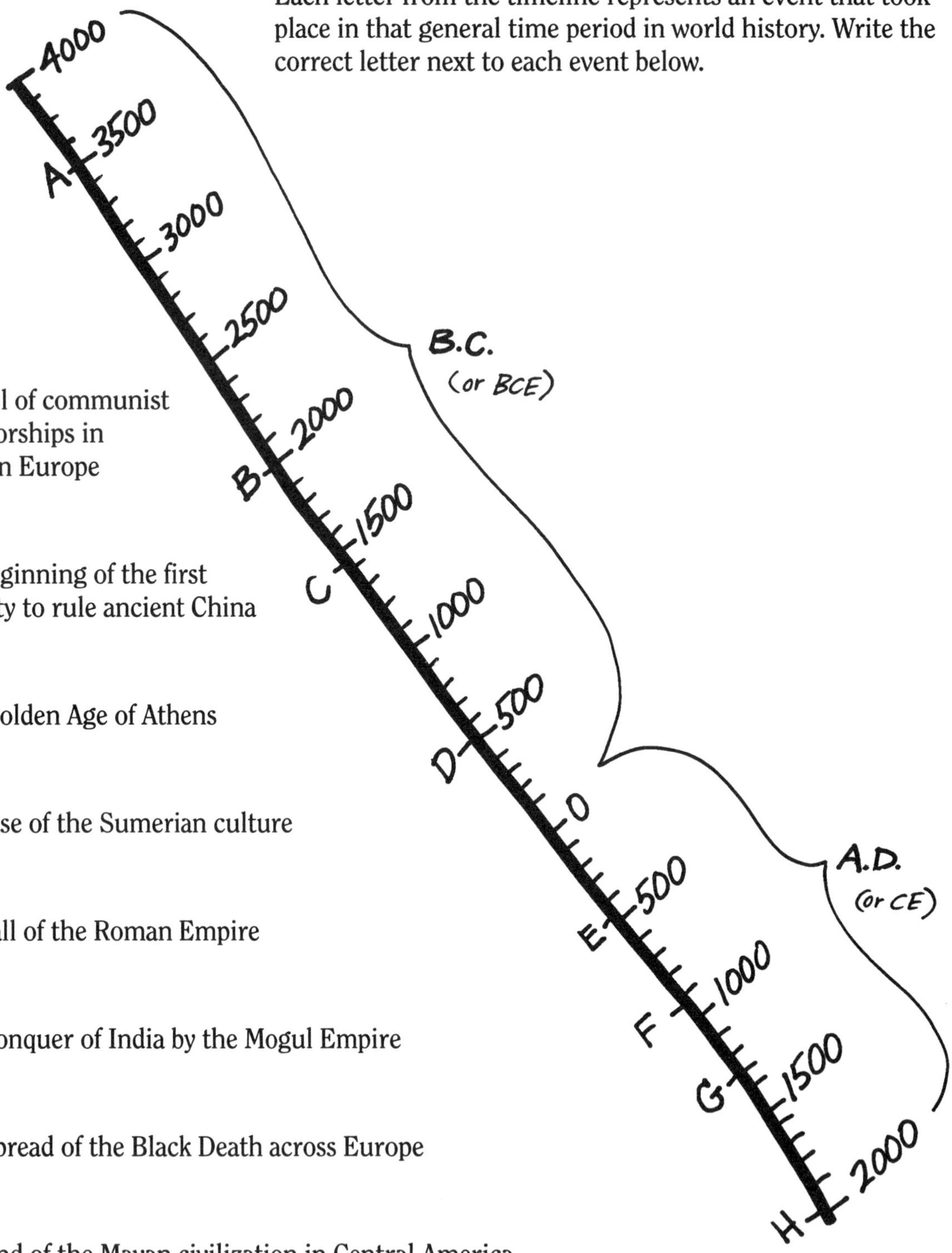

4000

A 3500

3000

2500

B.C.
(or BCE)

B 2000

1500

C

1000

500

D

0

500

E

A.D.
(or CE)

1000

F

1500

G

2000

H

_____ 43. the fall of communist dictatorships in eastern Europe

_____ 44. the beginning of the first dynasty to rule ancient China

_____ 45. the Golden Age of Athens

_____ 46. the rise of the Sumerian culture

_____ 47. the fall of the Roman Empire

_____ 48. the conquer of India by the Mogul Empire

_____ 49. the spread of the Black Death across Europe

_____ 50. the end of the Mayan civilization in Central America

Name _____

Choose the term that matches the description or definition.
Write the term on the line.

_____ 51. a 200-year period of peace
in the Roman Empire

_____ 52. a government in which
people choose their leaders

_____ 53. term for restructuring in the
Soviet Union under Gorbachev

_____ 54. conflict between people
in the same country

_____ 55. Muslim place of worship

_____ 56. political and economic system
of the Middle Ages

_____ 57. South African policy intended to
keep the races apart from each other

_____ 58. a rigid social class of Hindu society

Pax Romana

feudalism

republic

caste

civil war

empire

perestroika

oppression

mosque

apartheid

refugee

These are some of the events that caused change in the world.
Choose TWO, and explain the changes caused by each one.

59._____

_____

Industrial revolution
Renaissance
Break-up of U.S.S.R.
Invention of Tools
Irrigation
Arrival of Europeans in
Central America
Chinese Cultural Revolution
Invention of the Internet
Great Depression
American Revolution

60._____

_____

Middle Grade Book of Social Studies Tests

PEOPLE, PLACES, & ORGANIZATIONS

Name _____   Possible Correct Answers: 65

Date _____   Your Correct Answers: _____

Each of the names on Spike's list is an important person from world history.
Which person is associated with which event, organization, or situation in history?
Write a letter for each item. *(There may be more than one correct letter for an item.)*

Who is associated with . . .

_____ 1. the socialist party in Chile?

_____ 2. the first Greek university?

_____ 3. changes in South African policies?

_____ 4. the Holocaust?

_____ 5. the 1949 revolution in China?

_____ 6. the Vietnam War?

_____ 7. Soviet reforms in the 20th century?

_____ 8. the law of gravity?

_____ 9. the Roman Empire?

_____10. Renaissance art?

_____11. the Palestine Liberation Organization?

_____12. independence movements in South America?

_____13. the Korean War?

_____14. the Islamic religion?

_____15. the establishment of Israel?

_____16. the League of Nations?

_____17. fascism in Italy?

_____18. the French Revolution?

A. Marie Antoinette
B. Muhammad
C. Raphael
D. Joan of Arc
E. Ho Chi Minh
F. Woodrow Wilson
G. Galileo
H. Sandro Botticelli
I. Salvadore Allende
J. Golda Meir
K. Simon Bolivar
L. Yasir Arafat
M. Lyndon Johnson
N. F. W. DeKlerk
O. Mikhail Gorbachev
P. Aristotle
Q. Franklin Roosevelt
R. General MacArthur
S. Isaac Newton
T. Anne Frank
U. Julius Caesar
V. Mao Zedong
W. Nelson Mandela
X. Adolf Hitler
Y. Leonardo da Vinci
Z. Benito Mussolini

Middle Grade Book of Social Studies Tests   Copyright ©2001 by Incentive Publications, Inc., Nashville, TN.

Which person from world history fits the description?
Write a name for each quote.

19. *I am a German monk who led the Protestant Reformation.*

_____

20. *My paintings adorn the ceilings of the Sistine Chapel.*

_____

21. *As British Prime Minister during World War II, I led the fight against Hitler.*

_____

22. *I am perhaps the most well-known English playwright of the Elizabethan Renaissance.*

_____

23. *I led my Hebrew people out of slavery in Egypt on a 40-year journey back to our homeland of Canaan.*

_____

24. *As an explorer from Spain, I had the great thrill of being the first person to sail around the world.*

_____

25. *I am a German philosopher whose socialist ideas inspired the formation of communist governments.*

_____

26. *As a Hindu leader, I taught my fellow Indians to practice passive resistance as a form of civil disobedience.*

_____

27. *At age 16, I convinced the king of France to let me build an army. I led the army in many victories during the Hundred Years' War. I was captured by the English and burned at the stake.*

_____

28. *I am from Scotland, and best known because of my invention of the steam engine.*

_____

Name _____

83

Each letter on the world map shows the general location of one of these events in world history. Write the correct letter beside each event.

_____ 29. Japanese attack on Pearl Harbor

_____ 30. establishment of ancient civilizations in the Fertile crescent

_____ 31. arrival of Europeans into the Incan culture

_____ 32. symbolic site of the Iron Curtain

_____ 33. building of the Suez Canal

_____ 34. dropping of two atomic bombs

_____ 35. the Boer War

_____ 36. discoveries of explorer Samuel de Champlain

_____ 37. beginning of the American Revolution

_____ 38. signing of the treaty that ended World War I

_____ 39. rule of Kind Ferdinand and Queen Isabella

_____ 40. signing of the Magna Carta

_____ 41. success of the first communist revolution

_____ 42. the Opium Wars

Which country is described?
Write the name of a country for each description.

43. This country has a long history of hostility and fighting between Protestants and Roman Catholics.

_____

44. A great number of the settlers in this country in the 1700-1800s were prisoners who had been sent away from Britain.

_____

45. This country was invaded by Iraq in 1989. The invasion caused the United States to attack Iraq, beginning the Gulf War.

_____

46. From this country, Napoleon launched an empire that ruled most of western Europe in the early 1800s.

_____

47. Worker Lech Walesa, began the Solidarity Movement and struggled for this country's independence from Soviet control.

_____

48. Margaret Thatcher served as the first female prime minister from this country.

_____

49. Terrorists in this country took 53 American citizens as prisoners in the American Embassy, and held them hostage for over a year.

_____

50. Which did NOT happen in Athens?

   a. the building of the Parthenon

   b. the building of pyramids for rulers

   c. the writing of Socrates' ideas

   d. the formation of the first democracy

Name _____

85

Middle Grade Book of Social Studies Tests

Test items 51–58 describe topics of discussion that might take place at a meeting of one of the organizations below.
Write the name of the organization next to the discussion topic.

_____51. Members discuss distribution of funds to feed hungry children in the world.

_____52. Representatives of member European countries discuss elimination of trade barriers among their countries.

_____53. Representatives discuss plans to form an independent Palestinian state.

_____54. Members discuss ways to bring benefits of technology to all countries in the world.

_____55. Oil-producing countries discuss setting oil production levels.

_____56. Representatives of many countries discuss an issue of peace and security in an area of the world.

_____57. Members decide on an amount of money to loan a country in need.

_____58. Members discuss possible solutions for a major world health problem.

UN	UNICEF	EC or EU
UNESCO	WTO	IMF
WHO	OPEC	PLO

59. Which is NOT true of the League of Nations?

    a. U.S. President Woodrow Wilson proposed the League of Nations.

    b. It fell apart at the start of World War II.

    c. It was joined by every powerful nation in the world at the time.

    d. Its purpose was to prevent war.

60. What is the purpose of NAFTA?

    a. to eliminate trade barriers between the U.S., Canada, and Mexico

    b. to protect western European nations against military aggression

    c. to eliminate trade barriers throughout the world

61. What was the purpose of the SALT Treaties and discussions?

    a. to regulate the trade of salt in the world

    b. to distribute power after World War II

    c. to slow or stop the spread of nuclear weapons

62. Which countries were in the alliance called the Allied Powers in World War II?

    a. Great Britain, France, United States, Italy

    b. Great Britain, France, China, Soviet Union, United States

    c. Japan, Soviet Union, Germany, Italy

63. Which was the purpose of NATO when it was formed?

    a. to provide all the world's nations with a way to settle disputes peacefully

    b. to build U.S. and Western Europe in a common military defense against the Soviet Union and its Eastern European allies

    c. to promote trade between the U.S. and European countries

64. What alliance was formed as a protection against the NATO alliance?

    a. the Warsaw Pact   b. the Triple Entente

    c. the Axis Powers   d. OPEC

65. Which country was NOT a part of the Central Powers alliance in World War I?

    a. Russia   b. Germany

    c. Austria-Hungary   d. Turkey

Name _____

Middle Grade Book of Social Studies Tests

ANCIENT WORLD HISTORY

Name _____   Possible Correct Answers: 40

Date _____   Your Correct Answers: _____

Choose the correct term to match the description
of an era or event from ancient world history.

1. two invasions of soldiers from Asia Minor into ancient Greece
   a. the Trojan Wars
   b. the Persian Wars
   c. the conquests of Alexander the Great
   d. the Viking Raids

2. the era in Europe that followed the fall of the ancient Greek and Roman civilizations
   a. the Reformation   b. the Middle Ages   c. the Renaissance   d. Pax Romana

3. long period of peace in the Roman Empire
   a. the Dark Ages   b. the Reformation   c. Pax Romana   d. the Exodus

4. time during which democracy became the foundation of government in ancient Greece
   a. Age of Revolution   b. Middle Ages   c. Age of Pericles

Choose A, B, C, D, or E to match each of the historical time periods described below.

_____5. This period of time is thought of as the first stage
of known human life. People made tools from stone
and discovered how to use fire.

_____6. Features of this period of time in history are:
the domestication of animals, the beginning of crop
cultivation, and the establishment of villages.

_____7. During this period of time in history,
large sheets of ice covered parts of the earth.

A. The Ice Age

B. The Old Stone Age

C. The New Stone Age

D. Ancient Roman Civilization

E. Ancient Mesopotamian Civilization

Does Aristotle Rat have his facts straight about important persons in ancient history?
Circle the number of the correct items.
If he does NOT have it right, draw a box around the CORRECT answer.

8. Which great general from Carthage crossed the Alps with his troops
   and nearly ended the spread of the great Roman Empire?
   - **a.** Constantine
   - b. Napoleon
   - c. Hannibal
   - d. Alexander

9. Who was a blind poet that wrote great epic
   poems about adventures in Greek civilization?
   - a. Socrates
   - **b.** Homer
   - c. Euripides
   - d. Aristotle

10. Who was a leader of the Hebrew people who
    guided them out of slavery in Egypt?
    - **a.** Moses
    - b. Herodotus
    - c. Pharaoh Khufu
    - d. Solomon

11. Who was responsible for the spread of
    Greek ideas throughout a vast empire?
    - a. Abraham
    - b. Charlemagne
    - c. Alexander the Great
    - **d.** Plato

12. What Greek philosopher started the first university?
    - **a.** Aristotle
    - b. Euclid
    - c. Hippocrates
    - d. Sappho

13. What Arabian conqueror, who believed he was
    a messenger from God, led an army that captured
    Mecca in 630?
    - a. Julius Caesar
    - b. Omar Khayyam
    - **c.** Muhammad
    - d. Alexander

Name

89

Do you know the locations of the ancient civilizations?
Write the letter from the map that shows the location of each of the civilizations below.

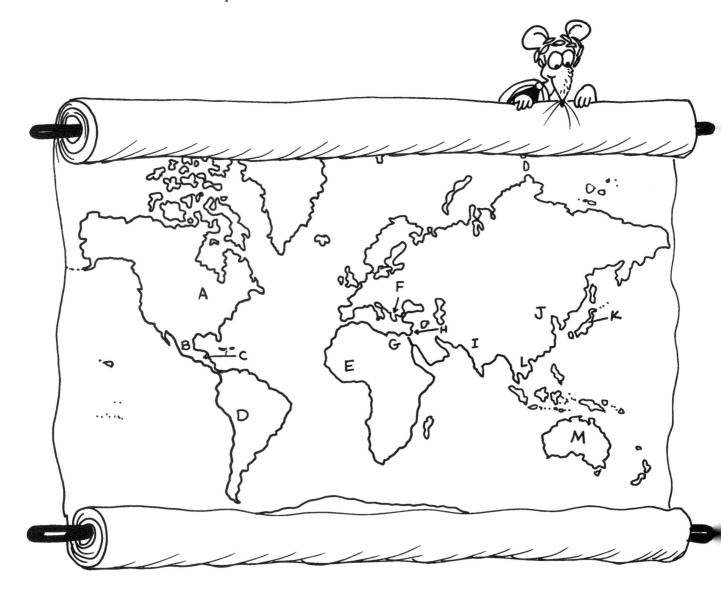

_____ 14. Shang Civilization

_____ 15. Ancient Greek Civilization   _____ 19. Mayan Civilization

_____ 16. Great Empire of Ghana   _____ 20. Ancient Egyptian Civilization

_____ 17. Incan Civilization   _____ 21. Mesopotamian Civilizations

_____ 18. Indus Valley Civilization   _____ 22. Aztec Civilization

Name _____

23. Which ancient civilization flourished in the Nile River Valley?

    a. Mesopotamian   b. Egyptian   c. Sumerian   e. Indian

24. Which of the following statements about ancient Egyptian civilization is NOT true?
(Circle one or more answers.)

    a. Agriculture was the basis of the ancient Egyptian economy.

    b. Ancient Egypt was one of the first societies to have an organized government.

    c. The ancient Egyptian civilization ended when their lands were conquered by Rome.

    d. The ancient Egyptians traded extensively with faraway places.

    e. Ancient Egyptian culture was recorded with a system of writing.

    f. Religion was not very important in ancient Egyptian culture.

    g. Ancient Egyptians believed in life after death.

    h. All members of the society were considered of equal value and importance.

    i. Ancient Egyptians were great builders, farmers, scientists, and artisans.

25. Mesopotamian civilization grew up in an area known as

    a. the Indus River Valley.   b. the Fertile Crescent.   c. the Nile River Valley.

26. Which of these modern-day countries occupies the area known as the fertile crescent?

    a. Egypt   b. Algeria   c. Iraq   d. India

27. Which of these statements is NOT true of the ancient Mesopotamian civilization?

    a. The Sumerian society had a strong central government.

    b. The Sumerians worshipped gods whom they believed would protect their cities and crops.

    c. The Sumerians invented a form of writing called *cuneiform*.

    d. Babylonian nomads conquered Sumer and adopted civilized Sumerian ways.

28. Each Sumerian city was the center of a political unit known as a _____.

29. Mesopotamia means the land between two rivers. Between which two rivers did the ancient Mesopotamian civilization flourish?

_____

        Middle Grade Book of Social Studies Tests

30. Which is NOT true about the history of the ancient Hebrew people?

a. Their leader, Abraham, led them across the desert to a homeland, called Canaan, located in the Fertile Crescent area.

b. They went to Egypt to find food during a famine, and were held as slaves for 400 years.

c. They followed a set of laws known as the *Code of Hammurabi.*

d. They believed in one God.

e. One of the world's greatest religions, Judaism, developed among them.

33. What modern-day country is in the area occupied by the ancient Indus River civilization?

a. China   b. Turkey   c. Egypt

d. Pakistan   e. Algeria

31. Scientists have discovered many artifacts from the ancient Indus River civilizations. Which of these is NOT shown by the artifacts?

a. The people built very large cities.

b. The people were highly skilled.

c. The people were traders.

d. The people were vicious and war-like.

e. They had built paved streets in their cities.

f. The people communicated with drawings and a form of writing.

34. Which statement is NOT true of the ancient Greek civilization?

a. The ancient Greeks were excellent sailors.

b. They left a rich cultural heritage of art, philosophy, theater, and literature.

c. They were committed to monarchy as the best form of government.

d. Athens became the first democracy.

32. Which is NOT true of the ancient Chinese civilizations?

a. A civilization grew up along the Huang River.

b. Villagers endured hardships of terrible floods.

c. The powerful Shang family united the villages of the river valley.

d. The family unit was not important in governing their society.

e. They believed that the spirits of their ancestors affected their daily lives.

f. They developed a system of writing.

35. Which of these is NOT true of the ancient Roman civilization?

a. Through the spread of the Roman Empire, the Latin language reached far across Europe.

b. The Romans were great architects.

c. Rome built a powerful empire by military might.

d. Rome ruled a large part of the Mediterranean region.

e. In wars with the colony of Carthage, the forces of Hannibal defeated Rome.

Name

92

Read the descriptions of three ancient civilizations in Latin America.
Match the name of the civilization to each description by writing A, B, or C.

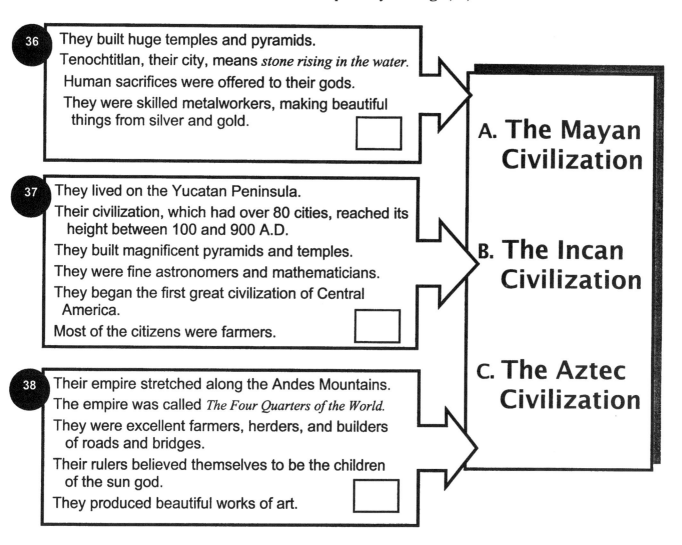

36 They built huge temples and pyramids.
Tenochtitlan, their city, means *stone rising in the water*.
Human sacrifices were offered to their gods.
They were skilled metalworkers, making beautiful things from silver and gold.

A. The Mayan Civilization

37 They lived on the Yucatan Peninsula.
Their civilization, which had over 80 cities, reached its height between 100 and 900 A.D.
They built magnificent pyramids and temples.
They were fine astronomers and mathematicians.
They began the first great civilization of Central America.
Most of the citizens were farmers.

B. The Incan Civilization

38 Their empire stretched along the Andes Mountains.
The empire was called *The Four Quarters of the World*.
They were excellent farmers, herders, and builders of roads and bridges.
Their rulers believed themselves to be the children of the sun god.
They produced beautiful works of art.

C. The Aztec Civilization

39. Which event happened first in ancient world history?

   a. Alexander the Great spread Greek ideas through a vast empire.

   b. Sumerian civilization grew strong in the Fertile Crescent.

   c. People discovered how to use irrigation.

   d. People discovered how to make and use tools.

40. Which event happened last in ancient world history?

   a. the beginning of democracy

   b. the fall of Rome

   c. the building of the Great Sphinx

   d. the Trojan Wars

Name _____

Middle Grade Book of Social Studies Tests

MEDIEVAL & MODERN WORLD HISTORY

Name _____   Possible Correct Answers: 50

Date _____   Your Correct Answers: _____

1. What is true of the Middle Ages? (Circle one or more answers.)
    a. The period lasted from about 500–1500 A.D.
    b. It followed years of brutal raids of Europe by Vikings.
    c. It brought a kind of organization back to European society.
    d. The Catholic church had very little power or influence.
    e. People lived inside manors to keep safe from attacks.
    f. It was called the Dark Ages because there was little emphasis on art or growth.
    g. Life in the Middle Ages was harsh for most people.
    h. Trade developed between Europe and the Middle East.

2. What is true of **feudalism**? *(Circle one or more answers.)*
    a. Feudalism encouraged great disorganization in the society.
    b. Most of feudal life was centered around the manor.
    c. The system was a way of organizing and governing society.
    d. The king granted land to nobles in exchange for their loyalty and services.
    e. Most of the people were serfs who lived and worked on land belonging to the nobles.
    f. Outside the manors, there were several towns and cities across Europe.

3. What is true of the Renaissance? (Circle one or more answers.)
    a. There was a great revival of interest in classic literature of Rome and Greece.
    b. The increase in trade began because of the travel involved in the Crusades.
    c. Rich families, called patrons, supported artists as they created works of art.
    d. The Renaissance began in England and spread across Europe.
    e. The Renaissance began in Italy and spread across Europe.
    f. The Renaissance encouraged freedom of thought, which likely inspired the birth of the Reformation.

Find the question that matches each answer below.
Write the letter of the correct question.

_____ 4. It is the extension of a country's power over other lands
by means of military, economic, or political power.
European countries spread their control to colonies all
over Africa, Asia, and the Americas during this period.

_____ 5. King John of England had increased taxes and angered
the people of England so much that they demanded
limitations on his power and more rights for the people.

_____ 6. Each was an organization of people who
performed the same craft or skill. They were
formed to control trade.

_____ 7. The purpose was to take control of the Holy Land
(Palestine) back from the Muslim Turks.

_____ 8. The purpose was to discuss reforms in practices of
the Roman Catholic Church and to make its teachings
more clear.

_____ 9. Parents paid a master to teach a skill to their child. The
child lived with the master and worked without pay.

_____ 10. They were places where learning continued. Books
were preserved in libraries and manuscripts were
copied by hand.

A. Why were guilds formed?

B. What is an apprentice?

C. What is imperialism and how does the term relate to Europe in this period of history?

D. What important societal function carried on in the monasteries during the Middle Ages?

E. Why was the Magna Carta written?

F. What was the purpose of the Crusades?

G. What was the purpose of the Council of Trent?

H. How did the Viking Raids affect Europe?

Name _____

Match the dates on the timeline to the events below. Write the date next to the event.

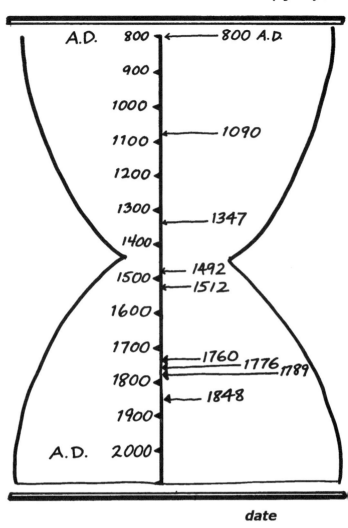

A.D. 800 ← 800 A.D.
900
1000
1100 ← 1090
1200
1300 ← 1347
1400
1500 ← 1492
← 1512
1600
1700 ← 1760 1776 1789
1800 ← 1848
1900
A.D. 2000

date

11. Marx & Engels publish *The Communist Manifesto*.

12. The First Crusade begins.

13. Marco Polo returns from his long trip to China.

14. Martin Luther nails a list of protests to a church door.

15. The American Revolution begins.

16. The Black Death begins its spread across Europe.

17. The French Revolution begins.

18. Christopher Columbus sails to the Americas.

19. Charlemagne is crowned emperor of Europe by the pope.

Name _____

96

20. Which was NOT a factor that affected the beginning of the Reformation?

    a. Martin Luther was outraged by Church practices such as the selling of pardons from the pope.

    b. Luther took back his protests when Pope Leo X threatened to expel him from the Church.

    c. Luther posted a list of protests on the door of a church in Wittenburg, Germany.

    d. The invention of the printing press increased the spread of Luther's ideas.

    e. The Roman Catholic Church had been extremely powerful during the Middle Ages.

    f. Martin Luther left the Catholic Church, as did millions of other people.

    g. The Church itself began a process of reform as a result of Luther's actions.

21. Which of these factors contributed to the Industrial Revolution in England?
(Circle one or more answers.)

    a. The country had a large work force.

    b. Technology improved spinning wheels.

    c. Rich merchants set up large machines and created factories.

    d. The invention of the steam engine made available a source of power for factories.

    e. The Industrial Revolution in America spread to England.

22. During the Industrial Revolution, the growing social class of factory workers became known as

    a. the middle class   b. the upper class   c. the ruling class   d. the working class

Match the European power
with the colonized areas.

Write the country that
colonized the areas below.

_____ 23. Brazil

_____ 24. Colombia, Mexico

_____ 25. Canada, India, Kenya

_____ 26. Congo

Britain

Spain

Portugal

France

?

Middle Grade Book of Social Studies Tests

Who's Who in history? Choose the person to fit the description.
Write the correct letter for each description.

_____27. King of the Franks from 768-814, he doubled the size of the Frank kingdom and was crowned emperor by Pope Leo III

_____28. A monk who set down strict rules for monasteries in the Middle Ages

_____29. King who governed France during the French Revolution, and was killed during the *Reign of Terror*

_____30. French leader who expanded the French Empire after the French Revolution

_____31. Tsar of Russia who helped bring the Industrial Revolution to Russia and expanded Russia's land holdings in the 1700s

_____32. Russian leader who took over the government in 1917 and began to build the new communism in Russia

_____33. Leader of the fight for independence from Spanish rule in Argentina and Peru

_____34. First European to sail around the Cape of Good Hope at the tip of southern Africa

_____35. Explorer who discovered an all-water route to India

_____36. Spanish explorer who discovered the Pacific Ocean

_____37. Inventor of the printing press that created a turning point in book production during the Renaissance

_____38. Scientist who proved the theory that the sun is the center of the universe

_____39. American inventor of the cotton gin

A. Louis XVI
B. Lenin
C. Gutenberg
D. Catherine the Great
E. Napoleon
F. Eli Whitney
G. Charlemagne
H. Vasco de Balboa
I. Galileo
J. Bartholomeu Dias
K. Henry the Navigator
L. Vasco da Gama
M. Benedict
N. Jose de San Martin

Name _____

How is Spike doing on his history test? Check his answers.
Circle the numbers of the items he has answered correctly.

HISTORY TEST

Name *Spike*

Read the statements about world history.
Write **T** for statements that are TRUE and **F** for statements that are FALSE.

F 40. About 1100-1800, the Kingdom of Zimbabwe flourished in Africa.

F 41. By 1700, most of Africa had been colonized by European powers.

T 42. South Africa was under Spanish rule for many years.

T 43. In the 1440s, the Portuguese brought Africans to Europe as slaves because workers were needed to replace those who died from the Black Death.

T 44. In the Great Trek, Afrikaners moved from central and eastern Africa into South Africa.

T 45. In the 1950s, General Abdel Nasser became the first Egyptian to rule the country in over 1000 years.

F 46. The Manchu Dynasty was the last dynasty to rule China.

F 47. In the late 1600s, Japanese rebels overthrew the ruling Shogun, and Japan began to build a modern empire.

T 48. In the mid 1400s, the Ottomans established a Muslim Empire that lasted into the 20th Century.

T 49. The great civilizations of the Aztecs and Incas were destroyed when Spanish soldiers took over control of the cultures from the native peoples.

T 50. Canada became completely independent of England in 1867.

MODERN WORLD HISTORY

Name _____   Possible Correct Answers: 55

Date _____   Your Correct Answers: _____

A student of history describes some of the major events of twentieth century world history.
What should he say?
Write a brief phrase or statement that describes each event or explains its importance.

1. Tianamen Square_____

2. Apartheid _____

3. Chinese Cultural Revolution_____

4. NAFTA Agreement_____

5. Berlin Wall_____

6. Sputnik_____

7. Pearl Harbor_____

8. 1972 Munich Olympics_____

9. Bay of Pigs Incident_____

10. Fall of the Berlin Wall_____

11. Iran Hostage Crisis_____

12. Holocaust_____

Read the descriptions of some major conflicts and agreements in world history.
Choose the correct letter from one of the boxes to match each description.

_____ 13. 1990-1991 U.S and UN response to Iraq's aggression against Kuwait

_____ 14. struggle between democracy and communism after World War II

_____ 15. 1950 war which began when communist forces in the northern part of a divided country invaded the south

_____ 16. 1900 rebellion by Chinese nationalists against foreign controls in their territory

_____ 17. 1967 war between Israel and Arab states over land in the Middle East

_____ 18. 1992 civil war between different ethnic groups over control of their newly-independent eastern European country

_____ 19. struggle in which the U.S. became involved in 1965 to stop the spread of communism through Southeast Asia

_____ 20. Agreement among Allied forces at the end of World War II as to the divisions and control of Europe

_____ 21. 1955 military alliance between the Soviet Union and other Eastern European nations to defend against West Germany and other members of NATO

_____ 22. Agreements between the U.S. and U.S.S.R. over the regulation of nuclear weapons

_____ 23. Agreement ending the war in Bosnia

_____ 24. Treaty ending World War I

_____ 25. 1978 Framework for peace in the Middle East

_____ 26. Agreement to share governmental control between Catholics and Protestants in a European country

_____ 27. 1949 defense alliance between U.S. and several western European nations to assure security and protect against attack from other nations

CONFLICTS
A. Six-Day War
B. Boxer Rebellion
C. Cold War
D. Vietnam War
E. Gulf War
F. Korean War
G. War in Bosnia

AGREEMENTS
H. Camp David Accords
I. Versailles Treaty
J. NATO
K. Warsaw Pact
L. Dayton Accord
M. SALT Agreements
N. Yalta Conference
O. Northern Ireland Peace Agreement

Name

101

28. Which was NOT a cause of World War I?

   a. Many nations began building up supplies of weapons.

   b. Countries formed alliances to protect against aggression.

   c. Industrialized powers in Europe wanted to expand the sizes of their empires.

   d. A lack of national pride and loyalty led nations to form alliances with other nations.

   e. Austria-Hungary attacked Serbia in response to the assassination of Archduke Ferdinand.

29. Which was NOT a result of World War I?

a. The United Nations was formed as a way to prevent another world war.

b. The size of Germany's army was reduced.

c. Germany was forced to give up territory to other European countries.

d. Germany was required to pay large sums of money in damages to other countries.

e. Germany was forbidden to have aircraft and submarines.

30. Which was NOT a cause of World War II?

   a. The Axis Powers wanted to conquer their neighbors.

   b. The Treaty of Versailles failed to bring a lasting peace to Europe.

   c. Fascist governments were rising in Germany, Japan, and Italy.

   d. Britain attacked Germany to stop the build-up of German weapon supplies.

   e. Worldwide depression and German nationalism fueled Hitler's rise to power

31. Which was NOT a result of World War II?

a. The Cold War began.

b. The League of Nations was formed.

c. Millions of people lost their homes and homelands.

d. Millions of people were killed.

e. Germany was divided into two countries.

f. U.S. and Soviet Union became the two great world powers.

32. Which statement is NOT true of the Cold War period?

   a. The Berlin Wall was built as a division between the two German countries.

   b. The Soviet Union wanted to spread the communist system to countries in Eastern Europe.

   c. The U. S., Canada, and Western European countries formed NATO as a military alliance.

   d. Japan joined the U.S.S.R. and Eastern European countries in the Warsaw Pact.

   e. Great tension existed between the communistic and democratic political systems.

Name _____

33. The UN was more effective than the League of Nations because

a. just about all the world's nations, including the U.S., are members.

b. it has been willing to oppose aggression by countries, sometimes with military force.

c. no wars have occurred in the world to test its effectiveness.

d. there is a large UN army, ready at all times to fight aggression.

e. all the nations have veto power over the decisions of the other nations.

34. The Marshall Plan and the Truman Doctrine were plans to

   a. keep the United States out of European affairs.

   b. rebuild European nations after World War II.

   c. reduce the tensions created by the Cold War.

   d. rebuild American forces after World War II.

35. A main purpose of the European Community and the European Union has been to

   a. form a military alliance to protect nations against outside aggression.

   b. increase economic cooperation among the countries of Europe.

   c. promote free trade with countries around the world.

   d. establish a common European language.

   e. agree on policies to protect the environment in Europe.

36. *Glasnost* and *perestroika* are policies that are connected with

a. the Soviet Union's desire to spread communism through Eastern Europe.

b. the United State's plans to stop the spread of communism in Europe and Asia.

c. Mikhail Gorbachev's reforms of restructuring and openness in the Soviet Union.

d. the movement to reduce nuclear weapons in Europe.

e. the movement to increase Soviet nuclear power.

37. Which statements are true of the Commonwealth of Independent (CIS)?

a. The CIS is controlled by Russia.

b. Armenia, Kazakhstan, Moldova, Belarus, and Russia are among the members.

c. The organization was founded to promote cooperation on economics, foreign policies, crime fighting, and environmental protection.

d. The control of nuclear weapons is an issue of concern for the commonwealth.

e. Ukraine is not a member of the CIS.

Name

Middle Grade Book of Social Studies Tests

38.   Which statement is NOT true of Latin America in the late 20ᵗʰ Century?

a. Many of the countries have serious economic problems, with rising debts.

b. Military dictatorships have gradually given way to democratically elected governments.

c. Several countries have experienced political unrest.

d. In many countries, large numbers of citizens remain extremely poor and unemployed.

e. Peace and stability are no longer seriously threatened by drug trafficking.

39.   Which statements are NOT true of the Middle East in the late 20ᵗʰ Century?

a. Conflicts have ended between Israelis and Arabs since the 1978 Camp David Accord.

b. There has been a revival of Islamic fundamentalism.

c. Many people distrust the western powers such as the United States.

d. Severe conflicts remain over the issue of a Palestinian state for Arabs.

e. The Gulf War ended the power of Saddam Hussein and Iraq in the Arab world.

40.   Which statement is NOT true of Africa in the late 20ᵗʰ Century?

a. European colonial rule was weakened in Africa after World War II.

b. Most African nations had gained independence by the 1990s.

c. Independence for African nations was gained without bloodshed.

d. Many young African nations struggled with political instability, poverty, and disease.

e. Policies of racial segregation ended in South Africa.

41.   Which statements are NOT true of Asia in the late 20ᵗʰ Century?

a. Japan recovered quickly from World War II and became a world economic power.

b. Communism took a stronger hold in Southeast Asian countries.

c. There was strong economic growth in many Pacific Asian countries.

d. China increased trade with the outside world.

e. The Chinese government recognized Formosa as a separate nation.

42.   Which statements are NOT true of Europe in the late 20ᵗʰ Century?

a. Many democratic governments have replaced communist-controlled countries.

b. Strong ethnic conflicts in the former Yugoslavia resulted in brutal civil wars.

c. Russia lost all of its nuclear power and influence in Europe.

d. Many Eastern European countries have joined the European Union.

e. NATO disbanded as an alliance among European countries.

Name _____

Write the letter that shows the correct location on the timeline for each event below.

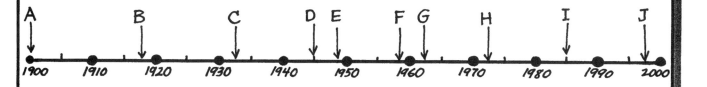

A   B   C   D   E   F   G   H   I   J

1900   1910   1920   1930   1940   1950   1960   1970   1980   1990   2000

_____ 43. The Cold War begins.   _____ 46. U.S. troops leave Vietnam.

_____ 44. Castro becomes dictator in Cuba.   _____ 47. Hitler rises to power in Germany.

_____ 45. Boxer Rebellion begins in China.   _____ 48. Soviet Missiles are placed in Cuba.

_____ 49. People's Republic of China is established.

_____ 50. Control of Hong Kong is returned to China.

_____ 51. Lenin takes over Russian government in Communist Revolution.

_____ 52. Gorbachev begins policies that lead to changes in the U.S.S.R.

53. Which began first?
   a. Cold War
   b. U.S. involvement in Vietnam War
   c. Korean War
   d. Six-Day War

54. Which came last?
   a. birth of democracies in Eastern Europe
   b. end of British control over Canada
   c. beginning of Apartheid in South Africa
   d. end of slavery in United States

55. Which came first?
   a. independence for India
   b. independence for Angola
   c. total independence for Canada
   d. independence for Lithuania

Name _____

   Middle Grade Book of Social Studies Tests

U.S History Skills Checklists

U.S. History Test # 1:

MAJOR ERAS & EVENTS IN U.S. HISTORY

Test Location: pages 109–113

Skill	Test Items
Identify and describe key events in U.S. history	1–8, 28–45
Explain the significance of selected events in U.S. history	1–8
Recognize general time period of events in U.S. history	9–11
Place events on a timeline	12–21
Describe and compare eras in U.S. history	22–27
Place events within eras in U.S. history	22–27
Recognize major conflicts in U.S. history	28–45
Understand causes and results of major conflicts in U.S. history	28–45
Recognize chronology of events in U.S. history	46–48
Recognize and describe changes caused by historical events	49–50

U.S. History Test # 2:

PEOPLE, PLACES, & ORGANIZATIONS IN U.S. HISTORY

Test Location: pages 114–119

Skill	Test Items
Identify key persons in U.S. history	1–17
Describe accomplishments of key persons in U.S. history	1–10
Connect key persons to an era in U.S. history	11–17
Recognize the state location of key events in history	18–31
Associate events or issues with state, city, or regional locations	32–37
Recognize the purpose of key organizations or agencies in U.S. history	38–49
Identify policies and programs in U.S. history and recognize their purposes	50–55

U.S. History Test # 3:

EARLY U.S. HISTORY THROUGH 1800

Test Location: pages 120–123

Skill	*Test Items*
Show understanding of the inhabitance of North America by indigenous Native American groups	1–2
Show understanding of the ways of life of the Native Americans	3–5, 7–9
Identify some groups of Native Americans	8
Show understanding of the changes brought to Native American life by the coming of Europeans to the continent	6
Identify key events and persons involved in the European explorations and discoveries in North America	10–14
Identify characteristics of different American colonies	15–23
Describe colonial life	21, 22
Describe reasons why various groups came to America	19, 23
Recognize causes and results of the French & Indian War	24–25
Recognize causes and results of the Revolutionary War	26–27
Explain the significance of quotes from the Revolutionary War period	28–30
Define unalienable rights	31
Understand some challenges faced by the new government	32
Recognize chronology of events surrounding the Revolutionary War; place events on a timeline	33–40

U. S. History Test # 4:

19TH CENTURY U.S. HISTORY

Test Location: pages 124–127

Skill	*Test Items*
Explain significance of events in 19th century U.S. history	1–8
Recognize key persons and events in the Westward Movement and expansion of the U.S. to the west; understand Manifest Destiny concept	1, 2, 4, 5, 6, 7, 22, 23
Recognize causes, results, and other factors related to the Civil War period	3, 10, 15, 17, 28
Recognize attitude of America toward European influence; describe Monroe Doctrine	8
Recognize causes and effects of various events in 19th century U.S. history	9–21
Identify results of the War of 1812	9
Recognize effects of the relocation of Native Americans	11, 23

Middle Grade Book of Social Studies Tests

Recognize some of the issues surrounding slavery in America 12

Identify events, people, and changes due to the rise of industrialism
   in the U.S. 13, 14, 20, 32–40

Identify key events and issues surrounding Reconstruction 16, 18, 19, 29

Recognize results of the Spanish-American War 21

Recognize events and issues from the Ages of Jefferson and Jackson 22–23

Recognize events and issues from the Age of Reform 24

Identify causes and results of the Mexican War 25–26

Describe benefits and problems brought on by the Industrial Revolution 30–31

Identify significant American inventors and inventions 35, 37, 38, 40

U.S. History Test # 5:

MODERN U.S. HISTORY SINCE 1900

Test Location: pages 128–133

Skill	*Test Items*
Identify key events related to modern America	1–7
Describe significance of events in modern U. S. history	1–7
Describe causes, results, and alliances of World War I	8–12
Identify causes and outcomes from conflicts in modern U.S. history	8–12, 16, 17, 19–22, 24, 27, 29, 30, 32, 33, 35
Describe features and events of the 1920s	13–15
Identify causes of the Depression	15
Describe causes, results, and alliances of World War II	16, 17, 19, 21
Identify programs of the New Deal	18
Identify events and effects of the Cold War	20, 24, 27
Identify location and results of the Korean War	22
Identify features of the Civil Rights Movement	23, 25, 26
Identify key events in post-World War II America	28–41
Identify issues related to the Vietnam War	29, 32, 33
Identify contributions of key persons in modern U.S. history	52–56
Recognize chronology of events in modern U.S. history	47–50

Middle Grade Book of Social Studies Tests

MAJOR ERAS & EVENTS IN U.S. HISTORY

Name _____   Possible Correct Answers: 50

Date _____   Your Correct Answers: _____

Consider the list that names some of the key events or issues in U.S. history.
Choose **EIGHT** (8) items.
For each one, write the letter of your choice, then write a phrase or statement that describes the event or explains its importance in the history of the United States.

A. Underground Railroad

B. U-2 Affair

C. Monroe Doctrine

D. *Bill of Rights*

E. The Confederacy

F. Louisiana Purchase

G. Pearl Harbor

H. Cuban Missile Crisis

I. Election 2000

J. Black Tuesday

K. The Roaring Twenties

L. Trail of Tears

M. Arab Oil Crisis 1973

N. Salem Witch Trials

O. Gold Rush

____ 1. _____

_____

____ 2. _____

_____

____ 3. _____

_____

____ 4. _____

_____

____ 5. _____

_____

____ 6. _____

_____

____ 7. _____

_____

____ 8. _____

_____

Middle Grade Book of Social Studies Tests   Copyright ©2001 by Incentive Publications, Inc., Nashville, TN.

Circle one or more answers for each question (9–12).

9. Which event or events did NOT occur during the period between 1600 and 1775?
   a. the formation of 13 new colonies
   b. the Mayflower Compact
   c. the Mexican War
   d. the Louisiana Purchase
   e. the French & Indian War

10. Which event or events did NOT occur during the period between 1800 and 1890?
   a. the Industrial Revolution
   b. the Abolition Movement
   c. the Great Depression
   d. Reconstruction
   e. the Civil War

11. Which event or events did NOT occur during the period between 1900 and 1950?
   a. voting rights for women
   b. Spanish-American War
   c. heavy immigration from Europe
   d. completion of Panama Canal
   e. Berlin Airlift

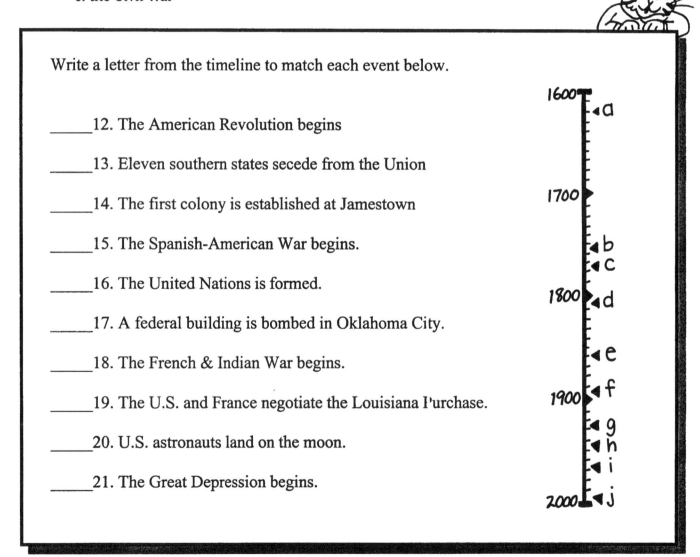

Write a letter from the timeline to match each event below.

_____ 12. The American Revolution begins

_____ 13. Eleven southern states secede from the Union

_____ 14. The first colony is established at Jamestown

_____ 15. The Spanish-American War begins.

_____ 16. The United Nations is formed.

_____ 17. A federal building is bombed in Oklahoma City.

_____ 18. The French & Indian War begins.

_____ 19. The U.S. and France negotiate the Louisiana Purchase.

_____ 20. U.S. astronauts land on the moon.

_____ 21. The Great Depression begins.

Name _____

Circle one or more answers for each question (22–27).

22. Which events occurred during the Revolutionary Period (1750-1783)?

   a. **Boston Massacre**
   b. **Declaration of Independence**
   c. **First Continental Congress**
   d. **Missouri Compromise**

23. Which events occurred during the period when the new nation was taking shape (1783-1850)?

   a. **Monroe Doctrine**
   b. **Election of Abraham Lincoln**
   c. **McCarthy Hearings**
   d. **Civil War**

24. Which events occurred during the period of Westward Expansion (1800-1900)?

   a. **Gold Rush in California**
   b. **Lewis & Clark Expedition**
   c. **Mexican War**
   d. **Spanish-American War**

25. Which events occurred during the period of the Industrial Revolution (1850-1900)?

   a. **Rise of Labor Unions**
   b. **Creation of monopolies**
   c. **World War I**
   d. **New Deal**

26. Which events occurred during the period of Civil War and Reconstruction (1860-1877)?

   a. **Rise of the Confederacy**
   b. **13th Amendment**
   c. **Lincoln assassination**
   d. **Lincoln-Douglas Debates**

27. Which events occurred during the Cold War era (1945-1985)?

   a. **Berlin Airlift**
   b. **Formation of the UN**
   c. **World War II**
   d. **Persian Gulf War**

Name

Each cause listed below is one of the factors that contributed to one of the wars on the chart.
Write the letter that matches the cause to show which conflict resulted.

CAUSES

_____28. Troops from North Korea invaded South Korea.

_____29. Britain and France were taking U.S. merchant ships.

_____30. The U.S. wanted the southern boundary of Texas to extend to the Rio Grande River.

_____31. American colonists were forced to keep British soldiers in their homes.

_____32. Germany invaded Poland.

_____33. U.S. states were divided over the issue of slavery.

_____34. The U.S. battleship *Maine* was sunk in a Cuban harbor.

_____35. Germany and Austria-Hungary, great powers in Europe at the time, wanted to expand their empires.

_____36. Iraq invaded Kuwait.

WHICH WAR?
A. American Revolution
B. War of 1812
C. Mexican War
D. Civil War
E. Spanish-American War
F. World War I
G. World War II
H. Korean War
I. Vietnam War
J. Persian Gulf War

RESULTS

_____37. Britain agreed to stay out of the Northwest Territory.

_____38. Many countries placed economic sanctions on Iraq.

_____39. Slavery was abolished in the U.S.

_____40. Widespread anti-war demonstrations broke out in the U.S.

_____41. The League of Nations was born.

_____42. U.S. gained all of California, Nevada, Utah, and parts of other western states.

_____43. Germany was divided into 4 parts.

_____44. The U.S. paid $20 million to Spain for the Philippines.

_____45. The fighting ended with no treaty, and a wide neutral zone between two parts of the country.

Name _____

Choose one answer.

46. Which came first?
   a. Cold War
   b. Vietnam War
   c. Korean War
   d. Persian Gulf War

47. Which came last?
   a. New Deal
   b. Boston Tea party
   c. Monroe Doctrine
   d. Great Society

48. Which came last?
   a. Women's suffrage
   b. Slavery outlawed
   c. Industrial Revolution
   d. Civil War

Indian Removal Act, 1830

Missouri Compromise

Fall of the Berlin Wall

Jim Crow laws

National Labor Relations Act, 1935

Sherman Anti-Trust Act, 1902

Brown v. Board of Education Court Decision

13th-14th-15th Amendments to the Constitution

*Choose two of the events from the list. For each one, write a paragraph explaining one or more **changes** that occurred as a result of the event.*

49. _____

   _____

   _____

50. _____

   _____

   _____

   _____

Name _____

Middle Grade Book of Social Studies Tests

PEOPLE, PLACES, & ORGANIZATIONS

Name _____

Possible Correct Answers: 55

Date _____

Your Correct Answers: _____

Who's who in American history? Write a name to match each description.

Clara Barton
Joseph McCarthy
Benedict Arnold
Harry Truman
Neil Armstrong
robber barons
Franklin D. Roosevelt
Frances Perkins
J. D. Rockefeller
Jane Addams
Dred Scott
Rosa Parks
Sandra Day O'Connor
sharecroppers
Robert Oppenheimer
Susan B. Anthony
carpetbaggers
Eleanor Roosevelt

_____ 1. The first female to be appointed to the U.S. Supreme Court.

_____ 2. U.S. physicist who headed the Manhattan Project which developed the first atomic bomb.

_____ 3. Social worker who worked hard to solve problems for people living in poor working conditions in cities during the Industrial Revolution.

_____ 4. American astronaut who was the first person to set foot on the moon.

_____ 5. Northerners who went to the south after the Civil War to make some profit from the unstable conditions.

_____ 6. American woman who fought relentlessly for a woman's right to vote.

_____ 7. U.S. senator who accused many prominent Americans and government workers of being communists.

_____ 8. American president who said, during his inauguration speech, ". . . the only thing we have to fear is fear itself."

_____ 9. First female cabinet member (Secretary of Labor under Franklin D. Roosevelt).

_____ 10. Black woman who refused to follow the law that required her to give up her bus seat to a white person, thereby sparking the Montgomery Bus Boycott.

Middle Grade Book of Social Studies Tests

Circle one or more answers (11-15).

11. Which of these people have some connection to the Westward Movement?

Robert E. Lee   *Thomas Paine*

Jim Crow   *Sacagewea*

Davy Crockett

Meriwether Lewis

12. Which of these people have some connection to the Industrial Revolution and the rise of the labor movement?

John D. Rockefeller **Samuel Gompers**

HENRY FORD   **Huey Long**

Dwight Eisenhower

Clara Barton   *Andrew Carnegie*

13. Which of these people have some connection to the Civil War period?

Harriet Beecher Stowe

Theodore Roosevelt

Ulysses S. Grant   Harriet Tubman

Thomas Jefferson

Stephen Douglas   **Dred Scott**

14. Which of these people have some connection to the period of colonial life or the American Revolution?

William Bradford

Ethan Allen   Benedict Arnold

Betsy Ross

George Washington   *William Penn*

Rosa Parks   **Thomas Paine**

15. Which of these people have some connection to the Cold War?

Josef Stalin   *William Clinton*

John F. Kennedy

Fidel Castro   Theodore Roosevelt

Joseph McCarthy   Nikita Khrushchev

Winston Churchill

16. The big businessmen of the late 1800s who became wealthy by driving small companies out of business (not always legally) were

  a. sharecroppers.   b. robber barons.   c. war hawks.   d. forty niners.

17. Citizens or government officials who wanted the nation to have little involvement with other countries were called

  a. contras.   b. imperialists.   c. isolationists.   d. internationalists.

Middle Grade Book of Social Studies Tests

Each star shows the location of an event national landmark.
Write the name of the state to match each item below. (Use the state's abbreviation.)

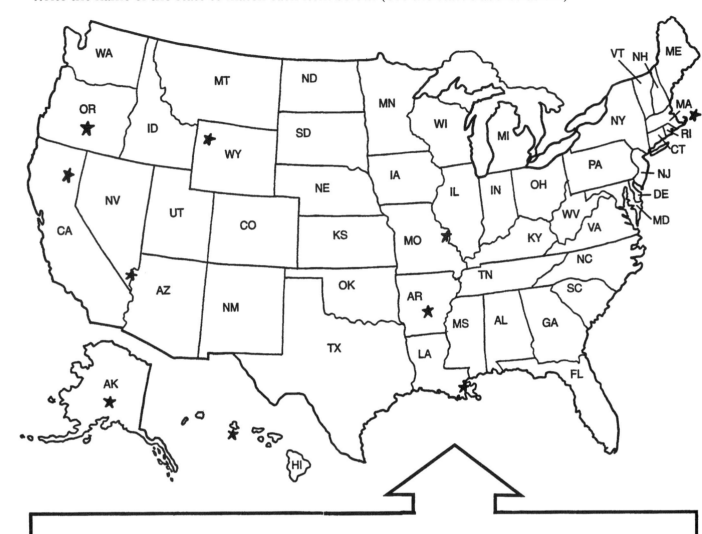

_____ 18. Attack on Pearl Harbor

_____ 19. 1857 purchase from Russia

_____ 20. Yellowstone National Park

_____ 21. last spike of Transcontinental Railroad

_____ 22. 1957 attempt to integrate a high school

_____ 23. beginning of trip on Oregon Trail

_____ 24. Object of *"54-40 or Fight"!* Campaign

_____ 25. Jamestown settlement

_____ 26. 1949 Gold Rush

_____ 27. Hoover Dam

_____ 28. Battle at Little Bighorn

_____ 29. Salem Witch Trials

_____ 30. Battle of New Orleans

_____ 31. Battle of Gettysburg

32. Which tobacco-producing colony, led by Lord Baltimore, was formed partly as a safe place for Catholics?

    a. Maryland   b. Massachusetts

    c. New Hampshire   d. New Jersey

    e. Georgia   f. Pennsylvania

33. Which territory was NOT gained by the United States at the end of the Spanish-American War?

    a. Puerto Rico   b. Cuba

    d. Philippines   c. Guam

34. Which area of the United States was the original homeland of these Native American tribes?
Apache, Navajo, Pueblo, Hopi, Mohave, Paiute, Taos, Yuma, Zuni?

    a. the north   b. the northeast

    c. the southeast   d. the plains

    e. the southwest   f. the northwest

35. A 1770 clash between British soldiers and Americans left several people dead or wounded. This incident occurred in

    a. Washington   b. Boston

    c. Philadelphia   d. Concord, New Hampshire

36. Which describes the location of the 1803 Louisiana Purchase from France?

    a. the present-day state of Louisiana

    b. the land from Florida west to the Mississippi River and north to the Ohio River

    c. all the land between the Mississippi River and the Rocky Mountains

    d. all the land west of the Rocky Mountains

37. Writer John O'Sullivan gave the name Manifest Destiny to an American attitude in the 1840s. Which idea was associated with that name?

    a. the desire of the Americans to become a world power

    b. the belief that the people of the United States could take over the whole continent

    c. the desire of many Americans to own Mexico

    d. the belief that slavery should be banned from new territories

Name _____

Middle Grade Book of Social Studies Tests

Write the name of the agency or organization that matches the description.

TVA

CIA

Central Powers

FDIC

ERA

Americorps

NOW

KKK

WTO

UN

AIM

NAACP

WPA

EPA

NASA

League of Nations

AFL-CIO

Peace Corps

NATO

FBI

_____38. formed to put an end to lynching of black Americans

_____39. created in 1947 to gather and interpret military, political, and economic information about other countries

_____40. combined two groups of labor unions

_____41. founded to work for fairer treatment of Native Americans

_____42. formed with goal of keeping black Americans from voting and having other power

_____43. established to monitor pollution and protect the environment

_____44. established in 1933 to develop water power resources and provide affordable electricity in the Tennessee Valley

_____45. created after the Great Depression to provide government insurance for peoples' bank savings

_____46. formed after World War II to help maintain world peace

_____47. responsible for space research programs

_____48. formed in 1966 to promote equal opportunity for women

_____49. formed by J.F. Kennedy for the purpose of sending volunteers to help people in needy countries

50. Which U.S. policy gave financial and military aid to nations for the purpose of helping them resist communism?
    a. the Truman Doctrine
    b. the Tonkin Gulf Resolution
    c. the Marshall Plan
    d. the Manhattan Project

51. Which was an agreement at the Constitutional Convention to create a House of Representatives and Senate elected by the citizens?
    a. the Compromise of 1850
    b. the First Amendment
    c. the Great Compromise
    d. the Camp David Accord

52. Which policy was passed to regulate labor union activities and outlaw unfair labor practices?
    a. the Atlantic Charter
    b. the Taft-Hartley Act
    c. the Doctrine of Nullification
    d. the Federal Securities Act

53. Which was the U.S. social and economic program of President Lyndon Johnson?
    a. New Deal
    b. Fair Deal
    c. Great Society
    d. New Frontier

54. Which was a decree by President Abraham Lincoln that freed the slaves?
    a. Emancipation Proclamation
    b. Declaration of Independence
    c. Gettysburg Address
    d. Freeport Doctrine

55. Which was President Kennedy's program to provide economic assistance for Latin American countries?
    a. Fair Labor Standards Act
    b. Works Progress Administration
    c. Alliance for Progress
    d. Emergency Quota Act

Name _____

EARLY U.S. HISTORY

Name _____   Possible Correct Answers: 45

Date _____   Your Correct Answers: _____

Write T (true) or F (false) for each statement.

_____1. The first Americans probably crossed onto the continent on a land bridge from Asia.

_____2. Humans probably did not inhabit North America until about 3000 years ago.

_____3. Early Americans had many different ways of living.

_____4. The activities of early Americans were strongly influenced by their environment.

_____5. Most Native Americans lived primarily by fishing.

_____6. All Native Americans were hostile to all the newcomers from Europe.

_____7. Most Native American nations or tribes lived by a set of strict rules under organized governments.

_____8. The Native Americans in the Northwest lived in pueblos built from adobe.

_____9. Native American life was organized and governed mainly by traditions and customs.

_____10. The discoveries of America were made by mistake by explorers looking for ways to get to China.

_____11. Prince Henry of Portugal contributed to exploration by starting a school for settlers wanting to live in new lands.

_____12. Christopher Columbus set out on his voyage to find gold and other riches.

_____13. After Magellan completed his around-the-world voyage, he took several other voyages of exploration.

_____14. After Balboa landed in Panama, he explored the area and accidentally ended up on the shore of the Pacific Ocean.

Middle Grade Book of Social Studies Tests   Copyright ©2001 by Incentive Publications, Inc., Nashville, TN.

Massachusetts
Rhode Island
Connecticut
New Hampshire
New York
New Jersey
Pennsylvania
Delaware
Virginia
Maryland
North Carolina
South Carolina
Georgia

15. first colony formed   _____

16. colony known as
New Sweden   _____

17. colony founded by
Puritan Roger Williams   _____

18. Quaker colony   _____

19. colony founded as a home
for people who could
not pay their debts   _____

20. colony known as
New Netherlands   _____

21. Most people in the _____ lived
on farms, growing grain crops. They also
manufactured leather goods, containers,
and ironworks.
a. New England colonies
b. Middle colonies
c. Southern colonies

22. **The Great Awakening** refers to _____
a. an interest in rebellion against England
among the colonies
b. a spread of religious feeling through the
colonies
c. an anger against the heavy taxes
imposed by England on the colonists

23. Which is NOT one of the reasons why colonists came to America?

a. to be able to own slaves
b. to gain political or religious freedom
c. to find riches
d. to make profit from trade
e. to find work
f. to gain freedom from debts
g. to gain adventure
h. to find a better life

Name _____

Middle Grade Book of Social Studies Tests

24. Which was not a cause of the French & Indian War?

    a. English colonists wanted control over French lands to make money in the fur trade.

    b. Britain and France were fighting in Europe and the war spread to the New World.

    c. A British general and his forces took control of Quebec, Canada.

25. Which was not a result of the French & Indian War?

    a. Spain got all French territory west of the Mississippi.

    b. France lost most of its power in North America.

    c. Britain gained control over Canada.

    d. Britain tightened its control on its own colonies.

    e. France kept control of New Orleans.

26. Which was not a cause of the Revolutionary War?

    a. Britain passed the Stamp Act, forcing colonists to pay heavy taxes on paper goods.

    b. Colonists in Boston were forced to keep British soldiers in their homes.

    c. Colonists protested taxes by dumping tea into Boston Harbor.

    d. Britain punished colonists with the Intolerable Acts.

    e. Militia groups of colonists fired shots at British soldiers in the new territories.

27. Which was not a result of the Revolutionary War?

    a. The United States kept only the land occupied by the original 13 colonies.

    b. Britain recognized the colonies as an independent nation.

    c. The United States of America was formed.

    d. Britain stopped control of American trade.

Explain the meaning and importance of each of these expressions from the Revolutionary War period.

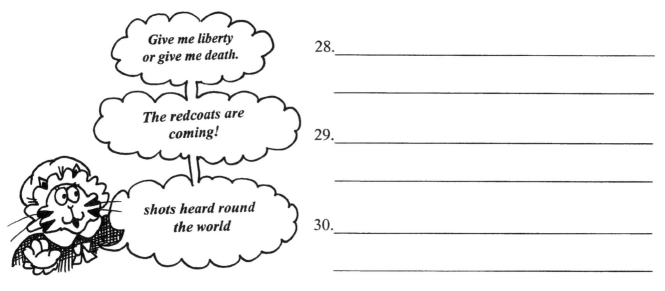

Give me liberty or give me death.

28._____

_____

The redcoats are coming!

29._____

_____

shots heard round the world

30._____

_____

The *Declaration of Independence* claims that all people are created equal, with certain ***unalienable rights.***

31. What is meant by unalienable rights?

_____

32. The first task after the Revolutionary War was to
    a. settle the question of slavery in the colonies.
    b. repair damaged relationships with Britain.
    c. build a strong army.
    d. create a new system of government.

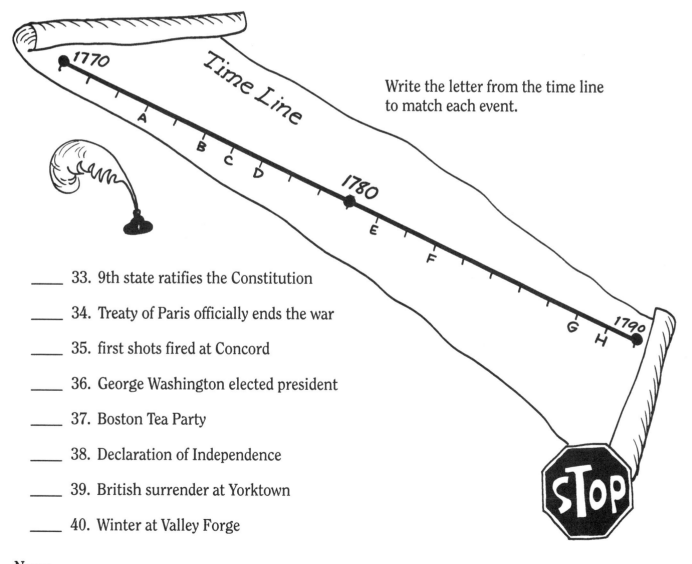

Write the letter from the time line to match each event.

____ 33. 9th state ratifies the Constitution

____ 34. Treaty of Paris officially ends the war

____ 35. first shots fired at Concord

____ 36. George Washington elected president

____ 37. Boston Tea Party

____ 38. Declaration of Independence

____ 39. British surrender at Yorktown

____ 40. Winter at Valley Forge

Name _____

Middle Grade Book of Social Studies Tests

19TH CENTURY U.S. HISTORY

Name _____

Possible Correct Answers: 40

Date _____

Your Correct Answers: _____

Each of these events, places, or documents has an important place in 19th Century history. Write a brief description for each one, and tell what effect it had on the country's history or the lives of its people.

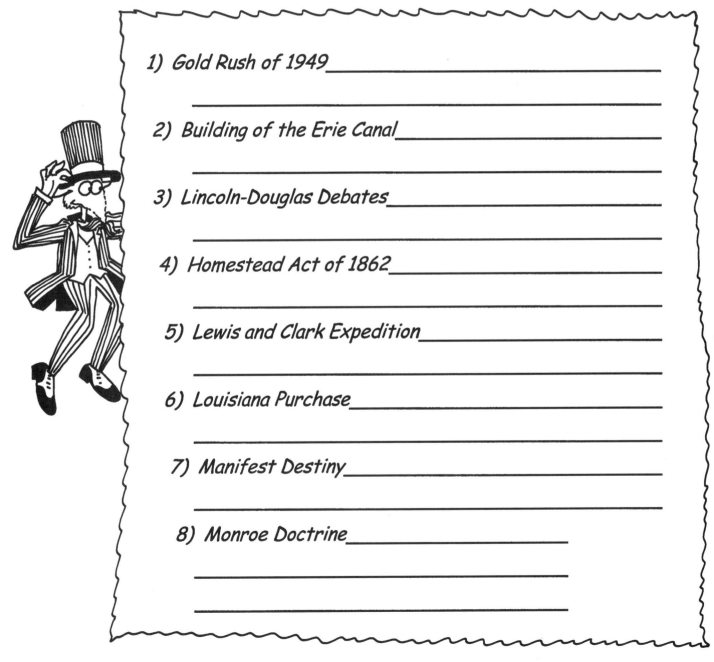

1) Gold Rush of 1949 _____

_____

2) Building of the Erie Canal _____

_____

3) Lincoln-Douglas Debates _____

_____

4) Homestead Act of 1862 _____

_____

5) Lewis and Clark Expedition _____

_____

6) Louisiana Purchase _____

_____

7) Manifest Destiny _____

_____

8) Monroe Doctrine _____

_____

_____

Middle Grade Book of Social Studies Tests

Copyright ©2001 by Incentive Publications, Inc., Nashville, TN.

For each cause listed, write the letter of an effect that resulted from that event.

CAUSES

_____9. the War of 1812

_____10. the election of Abraham Lincoln

_____11. the Indian Removal Act

_____12. need for labor on Southern farms and plantations

_____13. growth of monopolies in the nation's industries

_____14. poor treatment of workers in big companies

_____15. the Missouri Compromise

_____16. Jim Crow Laws passed in Southern states

_____17. victory of the North in the Civil War

_____18. disorder in the South after the Civil War

_____19. poor treatment of blacks after Reconstruction

_____20. expansion of the Industrial Revolution after the Civil War

_____21. the Spanish-American War

EFFECTS

A. Labor unions grew rapidly.

B. The British agreed to stay out of the Northwest Territory.

C. Thousands of slaves were brought to America.

D. Maine entered the Union as a free state.

E. Poor and unhealthy living conditions developed in many cities.

F. Many carpetbaggers from the North made profits during Reconstruction.

G. The Civil Rights Movement began and the NAACP was founded.

H. Native Americans were moved to reservations.

I. Separate areas were created for blacks and whites in public places.

J. Slavery was abolished and the Confederacy was dissolved.

K. Eleven states seceded from the Union.

L. The U.S. gained possession of Puerto Rico, Guam, and The Philippines.

M. Customers paid high prices for goods and companies made huge profits.

Name _____

125

22. Which would be associated with the Age of Jefferson? *(Circle one or more answers.)*

a. The Lewis & Clark Expedition

b. a strong belief in states' rights

c. the Louisiana Purchase

d. the addition of California as a free state

e. the end of Federalist power

f. Reconstruction

23. Which would be associated with the Age of Jackson? *(Circle one or more answers.)*

a. removal of Indians from their native lands

b. the War of 1812

c. increased influence of the "common man"

d. Manifest Destiny

e. addition of western territories

f. the Nullification Crisis

24. Which are characteristics of the *Age of Reform?*

a. There was progress in the fight to establish public education.

b. A movement began for expanding women's rights.

c. A movement to abolish slavery grew in strength.

d. Very few of the reforms actually took hold.

e. American writers and painters became part of the Romantic movement.

f. Reformers attacked social problems such as juvenile delinquency and mental health care.

g. Some reformers campaigned against the sale and manufacture of alcohol.

25. The Mexican War began because Mexicans and Americans disagreed about
   a. the ownership of Texas.
   b. the presence of slavery in southwest territories.
   c. the position of the border between Texas and Mexico.
   d. treatment of the Indians in the southwest.

26. What did Mexico give the United States in the treaty that ended the Mexican War?
   a. much of the land that is now Mexico
   b. most of the land in the present-day southwest
   c. Texas
   d. Texas and Oklahoma

27. Henry Clay is best known for

a. promoting compromise as a way to keep the nation together.

b. writing plans for Reconstruction after the Civil War.

c. overseeing the Lewis and Clark expedition.

d. forming plans for relocating Native Americans.

Name _____

Middle Grade Book of Social Studies Tests

Copyright ©2001 by Incentive Publications, Inc., Nashville, TN.

28. Which issues and factors led to the Civil War?

a. the treatment of Native Americans

b. different economic systems in the North and South

c. the election of Abraham Lincoln

d. slavery

e. the Gold Rush

f. states' rights

29. Which amendments and laws were parts of Reconstruction Legislation?

a. The 19th Amendment giving women the right to vote.

b. The Freedmen's Bureau was established.

c. The 13th Amendment freed the slaves

d. The 14th Amendment made all former slaves U.S. citizens.

e. Another amendment gave all black citizens the right to vote.

f. Force Acts protected blacks from terrorism.

30. Describe one benefit that the Industrial Revolution brought to the country.

_____

31. Describe one problem that the Industrial Revolution brought to the country.

_____

Write a letter to match the correct person to the description.

_____ 32. first leader of the AFL

_____ 33. big railroad businessman

_____ 34. controlled the Standard Oil Company

_____ 35. built the Model T

_____ 36. president who worked to break up trusts

_____ 37. found a cheap way to make steel

_____ 38. inventor of the telephone

_____ 39. founded a settlement house in Chicago

_____ 40. inventor of the light bulb and other inventions

A. Henry Ford

B. Jane Addams

C. Samuel Gompers

D. Cornelius Vanderbilt

E. Theodore Roosevelt

F. Thomas Edison

G. John D. Rockefeller

H. Henry Bessemer

I. Alexander Graham Bell

Name _____

127

MODERN U.S. HISTORY

Name _____

Possible Correct Answers: 50

Date _____

Your Correct Answers: _____

Consider the list that names some of the key events or issues in modern U.S. history.
Choose **seven (7)** items.

For each one, write a phrase or statement that describes the event or explains its importance in the history of the United States.

Panama Canal

Stock Market Crash

Bonus March

Sacco-Vanzetti Case

D-Day

Containment Policy

Domino Theory

SALT Treaties

Iran-Contra Affair

Watergate Affair

Wounded Knee

Kent State University

8. Which was NOT a cause of World War I?

A. Many people in Europe wanted freedom from Austria-Hungary.

B. Fascism was getting stronger in Germany and Italy.

C. Countries in Europe had formed military alliances.

D. Powerful countries in Europe wanted to take over more land in the world.

E. British submarines had attacked several German ships.

F. Austrian Archduke Ferdinand was assassinated by a Serbian terrorist.

9. Which was NOT a result of World War I?

A. The League of Nations was born.

B. Austria-Hungary was taken over by Britain.

C. Germany's armed forces were reduced.

D. Germany gave up territory to France, Belgium, Denmark, and Poland.

E. Germany had to accept responsibility for the war.

F. Germany had to pay millions of dollars in damages.

G. Some territories became protectorates of Allied countries.

10. The United States entered World War I when

    a. Germans attacked American citizens in Europe.

    b. Germans sank British and American passenger ships.

    c. Austria-Hungary invaded Britain

    d. Germany attacked France.

11. After the war, the U.S. did not join the League of Nations because

    a. there was a strong feeling of isolationism in the U.S.

    b. the European nations did not invite the U.S. to join.

    c. the cost of joining was too expensive.

    d. the U.S. did not have enough military personnel to commit to the League.

12. Circle the countries that were part of the Central Powers in World War I.

Belgium   Turkey   Bulgaria

Austria-Hungary   FRANCE

Russia   Germany   Italy

United States

Name

13. Which of these is true of the 1920s? (Circle one or more answers.)

    a. American businesses were expanding to produce weapons for European countries.

    b. People had money because they were able to borrow and buy on credit.

    c. The American economy was booming.

    d. The decade had a spirit of fun and relaxation.

    e. There was a boom in art, music, and literature.

14. The view of women changed in the 1920s because

    a. many women were running for public office.

    b. of the work women had done during the war.

    c. the National Organization of Women gained power.

    d. the president had a powerful wife.

18. Which were NOT programs of the New Deal?

Federal Deposit Insurance Corporation
Agricultural Adjustment Act
Tennessee Valley Authority
Drug Enforcement Agency
Environmental Protection Agency
Social Security Administration
Fair Labor Practices Act
Homeowners Loan Corporation
Federal Emergency Relief Administration
National Farm Workers Association
Peace Corps

15. Which was NOT a cause of the Great Depression?

    a. over confidence in the economy

    b. investment in risky stocks

    c. production of more goods than were needed

    d. fear of another world war

    e. careless borrowing and lending of money

16. Which was NOT a cause of World War II?

    a. German humiliation after World War I

    b. National pride in Germany, Japan, and Italy

    c. Fascism in Italy and Germany

    d. Desire in Japan, Italy, and Germany to conquer their neighbors and expand empires

    e. Dropping of atomic bombs on Japan

17. The U.S. entered World War II when

    a. Germany invaded Poland.

    b. Italy invaded Africa.

    c. Japan attacked Pearl Harbor.

    d. the Allies decided to invade France.

    e. Germany fired on a U.S. ship off Iceland.

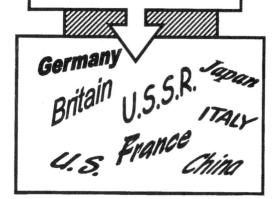

19. Which countries were part of the Allied Forces in World War II?

Germany
Britain U.S.S.R. Japan
ITALY
U.S. France China

Name _____

20. Circle the Cold War events.

NATO	Launch of Sputnik
Berlin Airlift	Bay of Pigs invasion
McCarthyism	Truman Doctrine
U-2 Affair	Cuban Missile Crisis
Korean War	Montgomery Bus Boycott
Iran-Contra Affair	Policy of Containment
Berlin Wall	Persian Gulf War
Tet Offensive	War in Bosnia
Vietnam War	Berlin Blockade
Domino Theory	Marshall Plan

21. Which leaders made decisions at Yalta about the future of Europe?

    a. Stalin, Chamberlain, and Truman

    b. Churchill, Roosevelt, and Stalin

    c. Churchill, Eisenhower, and Stalin

22. What was the outcome of the Korean War?

    a. North Korea gained more territory.

    b. South Korea gained more territory.

    c. Neither side gained more territory.

23. The Montgomery Bus Boycott and the sit-ins at lunch counters were examples of

    a. nonviolent resistance.

    b. terrorism.

    c. isolationism.

    d. compromise.

24. What policy affected the U.S. decision to get involved in the Korean War?

    a. *glasnost*

    b. Monroe Doctrine

    c. containment

    d. vietnamization

25. The organization that sprang up in the 1960s to organize campaigns for equal rights was

    a. the Student Liberation Army.

    b. the National Association for the Advancement of Colored People.

    c. the Southern Christian Leadership Conference.

    d. the Ku Klux Klan.

26. Which Supreme Court decision put an end to segregation?

    a. *Plessy v. Ferguson*

    b. *Brown v. The Board of Education of Topeka*

    c. *Schenk v. United States*

    d. *Dred Scott v. Sanford*

Name

Circle TRUE or FALSE for each question (27–36).

27. TRUE or FALSE?
The Domino Theory was based on the idea that if a communist government controlled South Vietnam, communism would spread to all its neighbors in Asia.

32. TRUE or FALSE?
From the beginning of the Vietnam War, and throughout the war, the U.S. followed the policy of vietnamization.

33. TRUE or FALSE?
The Vietnam War proved that the Domino Theory was true.

28. TRUE or FALSE?
All of these programs were part of Lyndon Johnson's Great Society Plan: Medicare, Head Start, VISTA, the Job Corps, and the Economic Opportunity Act.

34. TRUE or FALSE?
Ideas for expanding into new areas, such as space, were part of the program of The New Frontier program of President Ronald Reagan.

29. TRUE or FALSE?
The Vietnam War was supported by the citizens back in the U.S. and the returning soldiers were welcomed home as heroes.

35. TRUE or FALSE?
The Iran-Contra deal was a secret deal to sell arms to Iran in exchange for the release of hostages.

30. TRUE or FALSE?
Jimmy Carter lost the 1980 presidential election partly because of the Iran Hostage Crisis.

36. TRUE or FALSE?
The "Reagan Revolution" refers to a program to increase government programs to provide more services for the people.

31. TRUE or FALSE?
The Watergate Scandal came about because Republican campaign officials arranged for a break-in at the Democratic National Committee Headquarters.

Name _____

132

Write the letter of the matching description (37–46).

_____37. NAFTA

_____38. SALT

_____39. ERA

_____40. 26th Amendment

_____41. supply-side economics

_____42. Ruth Bader-Ginsberg

_____43. Elizabeth Cady Stanton

_____44. Langston Hughes

_____45. John Foster Dulles

_____46. Cesar Chavez

A. proposed Constitutional amendment that would guarantee certain rights for women

B. Treaty that limits the use of nuclear weapons

C. Constitutional amendment that lowered the voting age to 18

D. Theory that reducing taxes would create more investments, more profits, and thus supply more tax revenues.

E. Trade agreement between U. S., Mexico, & Canada

F. Organized the first Women's Rights Convention

G. Clinton appointee to the Supreme Court

H. Worker who began the National Farm Workers Association

I. Poet who wrote with pride and about the African-American experience

J. Powerful Secretary of State during the Eisenhower administration and early Cold War period

47. Which came first?
   a. Watergate Affair
   b. Roaring Twenties
   c. Black Tuesday
   d. Panama Canal

48. Which came first?
   a. Cold War
   b. Persian Gulf War
   c. War in Bosnia
   d. Vietnam War

49. Which came last?
   a. Manhattan Project
   b. Treaty of Paris
   c. Iran Hostage Crisis
   d. end of segregation

50. Which came last?
   a. U.S. troops leave Vietnam
   b. NAFTA
   c. Vietnam War protests
   d. first moon landing

Name _____

Middle Grade Book of Social Studies Tests

U.S. Government & Citizenship Skills Tests

U.S. Government & Citizenship Test # 1:

KEY U.S. DOCUMENTS

Test Location: pages 136–139

Skill	Test Items
Recognize the purposes and names of key U.S. documents	1–9
Discriminate between important U.S. documents	1–9
Understand concepts covered in key U.S. documents	2, 3, 5, 7, 9, 10–11
Recognize key ideas of the Declaration of Independence	2, 10, 11
Recognize key ideas of the Bill of Rights	22–28
Interpret meaning and importance of rights outlined in the Bill of Rights	23–28
Discriminate between parts of the Constitution; identify purposes of the different sections	29–34
Identify the significance of key amendments to the Constitution	35–40

U.S. Government & Citizenship Test # 2:

GOVERNMENT STRUCTURE & FUNCTION

Test Location: pages 140–145

Skill	Test Items
Show understanding of structure of the federal government	1
Show understanding of the concepts of separation of powers and checks and balances	1–5
Distinguish between the duties of the three branches of government	7–18
Identify duties and requirements of the executive branch	3, 5, 10, 13, 17, 18
Identify duties and requirements of the legislative branch	4, 5, 7, 8, 9, 11, 14, 15, 16, 31–42
Identify duties and requirements of the judicial branch	6, 12, 44–51
Describe members and duties of the President's Cabinet	19–30
Recognize process by which a law is made	42
Understand how a veto can be overridden	43
Identify some key Supreme Court decisions in U.S. history	52–56
Distinguish between different kinds of powers: enumerated, implied, inherent, reserved, concurrent, delegated	57–63
Identify powers that are federal, state, or shared powers	64–79
Show understanding of election processes	80–90

Middle Grade Book of Social Studies Tests

U.S. Government & Citizenship Test # 3:

OFFICIALS, AGENCIES, & INSTITUTIONS

Test Location: pages 146–149

Skill	*Test Items*
Recognize responsibilities of different officials of the government	1–9
Identify some U.S. presidents and events that took place during their administrations	10–22
Identify government officials of state and local governments	23–28
Identify some key institutions and their functions	29–30
Show understanding of some of the principles upon which the U.S. government is based	31
Identify the names and functions of key government agencies	32–45

U.S. Government & Citizenship Test # 4:

U. S. CITIZENSHIP

Test Location: pages 150–152

Skill	*Test Items*
Identify current government officials at the federal and local level	1–9
Show understanding of some significant event or issue in the history of one's own state	10
Show understanding voting rights and the voting process	11–15, 17,19, 22, 23
Show understanding of some responsibilities of citizens	16
Identify some responsibilities of officials in relationship to elections	20, 21
Recognize the location of national and historical landmarks or points of interest	24–26, 29–32, 34, 35
Show understanding and recognition of national symbols	27, 28, 33

KEY U.S. DOCUMENTS

Name _____   Possible Correct Answers: 40

Date _____   Your Correct Answers: _____

Match the correct document with its description.
Write the letter on the line.
A document may be used more than once.

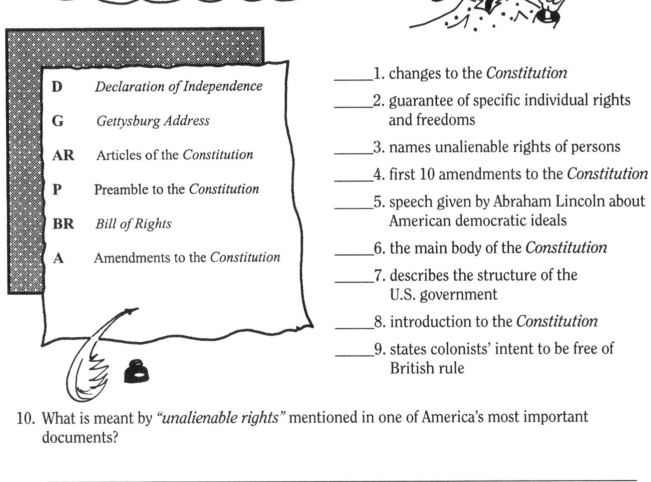

D   *Declaration of Independence*

G   *Gettysburg Address*

AR   Articles of the *Constitution*

P   Preamble to the *Constitution*

BR   *Bill of Rights*

A   Amendments to the *Constitution*

_____1. changes to the *Constitution*

_____2. guarantee of specific individual rights and freedoms

_____3. names unalienable rights of persons

_____4. first 10 amendments to the *Constitution*

_____5. speech given by Abraham Lincoln about American democratic ideals

_____6. the main body of the *Constitution*

_____7. describes the structure of the U.S. government

_____8. introduction to the *Constitution*

_____9. states colonists' intent to be free of British rule

10. What is meant by *"unalienable rights"* mentioned in one of America's most important documents?

_____

11. What are the specific "unalienable rights" that the document describes?

_____

Read each quote. Write the code letters to show which document is the source of the quotation.

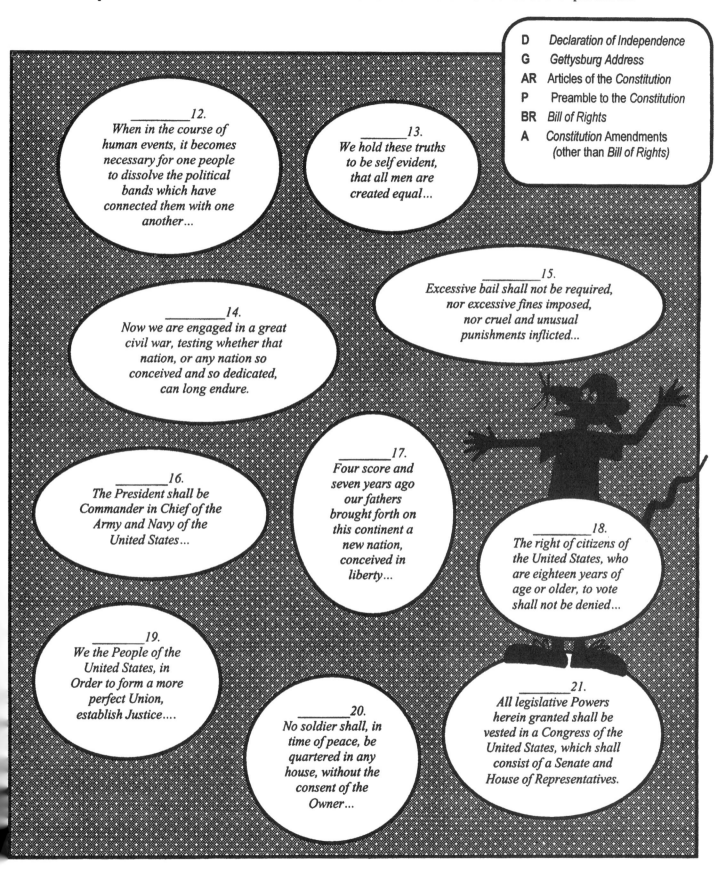

D Declaration of Independence
G Gettysburg Address
AR Articles of the *Constitution*
P Preamble to the *Constitution*
BR *Bill of Rights*
A *Constitution* Amendments (other than *Bill of Rights*)

_____12.
When in the course of human events, it becomes necessary for one people to dissolve the political bands which have connected them with one another...

_____13.
We hold these truths to be self evident, that all men are created equal...

_____15.
Excessive bail shall not be required, nor excessive fines imposed, nor cruel and unusual punishments inflicted...

_____14.
Now we are engaged in a great civil war, testing whether that nation, or any nation so conceived and so dedicated, can long endure.

_____16.
The President shall be Commander in Chief of the Army and Navy of the United States...

_____17.
Four score and seven years ago our fathers brought forth on this continent a new nation, conceived in liberty...

_____18.
The right of citizens of the United States, who are eighteen years of age or older, to vote shall not be denied...

_____19.
We the People of the United States, in Order to form a more perfect Union, establish Justice....

_____20.
No soldier shall, in time of peace, be quartered in any house, without the consent of the Owner...

_____21.
All legislative Powers herein granted shall be vested in a Congress of the United States, which shall consist of a Senate and House of Representatives.

Name _____

137

Middle Grade Book of Social Studies Tests

22. Which statements about the *Bill of Rights* are true?
    (Circle one or more answers.)
    a. The *Bill of Rights* was a part of the original *Constitution*.
    b. The *Bill of Rights* was added before the necessary nine states had
       ratified the *Constitution*.
    c. The people asked for a *Bill of Rights* because they were afraid
       the new government had too much power.
    d. The *Bill of Rights* was added after the *Constitution* was ratified.

Read the following imaginary scenes taking place in the United States today. For each
one, write a phrase that tells which right, guaranteed by the *Bill of Rights*, has been violated.

23. Sam has been accused of stealing a
car. He was arrested two years ago, and
is sitting in jail, waiting for a trial. No
one has told him anything about what
will happen next for him.

_____

26. A teenager was arrested for
shoplifting. This was the first time he
had been in any trouble. The judge
ordered that the teenager should be
whipped in the middle of the town mall.

_____

24. A citizen writes an angry letter to a
newspaper. The letter disagrees with a
new policy of the state government.
Police come to her house and arrest her.

_____

27. A group of army officers came
through a neighborhood at night and
demanded that all gun-owning citizens
turn over their guns immediately.

_____

25. A young lady was arrested and tried
by a jury for robbing a bank. The jury
found that she was innocent. Later, she
was arrested again, and put in jail for
the same crime.

_____

28. Abigail was walking to school,
doing nothing suspicious. She did not
break any laws or cause any trouble on
her way. A policeman stopped her and
searched her backpack.

_____

Name _____

Middle Grade Book of Social Studies Tests

Which part of the Constitution would apply to each of these?

_____ 29. A 45-year old woman, born in the U.S., decides to run for president.

> Write **P** for Preamble,
> **AR** for Articles of the Constitution,
> **BR** for Bill of Rights (Amendments 1-10),
> **A** for Amendments (other than 1-10).

_____ 30. A local newspaper prints what the editor decides is important to the people of his town without fear of government censorship.

_____ 31. Slavery will never again be allowed in the United States.

_____ 32. Congress has the power to borrow money for the United States.

_____ 33. It is the responsibility of the Executive branch of the U.S. government to make sure that citizens obey the law.

_____ 34. A citizen of Ohio cannot be asked to pay more federal taxes than a citizen from Iowa.

What rights were given to former slaves by the 13th, 14th, and 15th amendments?

35. _____

The 21st amendment repealed the 18th amendment. What did the 18th amendment prohibit?

36. _____

What did the 26th amendment change for voters?

37. _____

What did the 19th amendment guarantee for women?

38. _____

What change was made to the presidency by the 22nd amendment?

39. _____

What did the 16th amendment do that affected the country's economy?

40. _____

Name _____

Middle Grade Book of Social Studies Tests

GOVERNMENT STRUCTURE & FUNCTION

Name _____

Date _____

Possible Correct Answers: 90

Your Correct Answers: _____

1. A. What are the branches of the United States Government?

   _____

   _____

   _____

   B. What is meant by separation of powers?

   _____

   _____

   _____

2. The executive branch checks the legislative branch by
   a. vetoing bills
   b. changing laws
   c. impeaching the legislators
   d. setting congressional salaries

3. The legislative branch checks the executive branch by
   a. overriding the president's veto
   b. approving presidential appointments
   c. The House impeaching the president or vice president
   d. all of the above

4. The legislative branch checks the judicial branch by
   a. the Senate approving judicial appointments
   b. impeaching justices
   c. appointing justices
   d. answers a and b

5. The judicial branch checks the legislative branch by
   a. vetoing laws
   b. impeaching a senator or representative
   c. setting congressional salaries
   d. finding laws unconstitutional

6. Which job in the U.S. government is advertised here?

   _____

NOW ACCEPTING APPLICATIONS
Good-Paying Job
2-Year contract!
Long Hours
--Must be U.S. citizen
--Must be at least 25 years old
--Must be a resident of the state
--Must relocate for job

Middle Grade Book of Social Studies Tests

Copyright ©2001 by Incentive Publications, Inc., Nashville, TN.

Write a letter (see codes) to show which governmental branch or official has each of the powers below.

P = President
C = Congress
H = House of Representatives
S = Senate
SC = Supreme Court

_____ 7. coins money

_____ 8. levies taxes

_____ 9. can impeach an official

_____ 10. commands the armed forces

_____ 11. can override a veto

_____ 12. can declare a law unconstitutional

_____ 13. appoints justices to the Supreme Court

_____ 14. serves as a jury in an impeachment trial

_____ 15. ratifies treaties

_____ 16. approves appointments

_____ 17. can veto a law

_____ 18. acts as Chief of State

Which Cabinet Member?

Write the title of the Cabinet member who is responsible for each area described.

19. foreign affairs _____

20. educational issues _____

21. housing and cities _____

22. working conditions _____

23. money _____

24. legal issues _____

25. war veterans _____

26. U. S. lands _____

27. armed forces _____

28. business _____

29. roads _____

30. farming _____

Name _____

Middle Grade Book of Social Studies Tests

Which statements about Congress are true? Circle the numbers of all the correct statements.

FACTS ABOUT CONGRESS

31. The president of the Senate is the Vice President.

32. The Senate acts as a jury in an impeachment process.

33. Senators serve for a term that is six years in length.

34. There are 435 members in the House of Representatives.

35. The Senate has one member from each state.

36. The Congress meets in the White House.

37. The presiding officer of the House of Representatives is the Vice President.

38. The number of Representatives from a state depends on the state's size.

39. Only the House of Representatives has the power to begin impeachment proceedings.

40. Every two years, one-third of the body of the House of Representatives is up for election.

41. The Senate is the only branch of the legislature that can introduce bills to raise money.

42. **Number these in the order they would happen for a bill to become law.**

_____ If both houses pass the bill, it is sent to the president.

_____ The bill is introduced in both houses of Congress.

_____ The bill is passed by a majority of members in both houses of Congress.

_____ The president signs the bill into law.

_____ Committees in each house of Congress discuss the bill and change it if they wish.

_____ If the committee approves the bill, it goes to the full House or Senate for debate and vote.

_____ A member of Congress proposes a law.

43. Explain what happens to a bill if the president vetoes it.

_____

_____

_____

Name _____

Each statement about the justice system has an error. Change or replace words to make each statement correct.

44. There are 13 Supreme Court justices.	45. Supreme Court justices are appointed by the Senate and confirmed by the president.	46. As of 2001, there are no women serving on the Supreme Court.	47. Before the Supreme Court's decision is official, four members have to agree on it.
48. Once appointed to the Supreme Court, a justice cannot be removed.	49. The Judicial Branch passes laws.	50. The first major body of the judicial branch is the appeals court.	51. A Supreme Court justice serves for 12 years.

Match the court case with the correct description.

____ 52. ruled that anyone who is arrested must be read a statement of their rights before being questioned

____ 53. ruled school segregation unconstitutional

____ 54. ruled that a school cannot ban books from a school library just because someone does not agree with the ideas in them

____ 55. ruled that schools cannot require students to say prayers at school

____ 56. ruled that the government can't stop a person from a view or action (such as flag burning) because it is offensive

A. Miranda v. Arizona

B. Texas v. Johnson

C. Board of Education v Pico

D. U.S. v. Nixon

E. Plessy v. Ferguson

F. Brown v. Board of Education

G. Engel v. Vitale

Name _____

Middle Grade Book of Social Studies Tests

Write the letter to match the correct definition to the different kinds of powers.

_____ 57. enumerated powers
_____ 58. inherent powers
_____ 59. implied powers
_____ 60. reserved powers
_____ 61. concurrent powers
_____ 62. delegated powers

A. *powers given to the national government*

B. *powers held by the states*

C. *powers shared by the states and the federal government*

D. *powers that are clearly stated in the Constitution*

E. *general powers stated in the Constitution but not clearly outlined*

F. *unwritten powers that Congress must have simply because it is government and needs to run things smoothly*

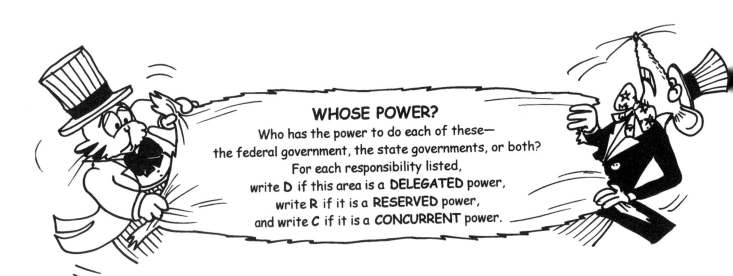

WHOSE POWER?
Who has the power to do each of these—
the federal government, the state governments, or both?
For each responsibility listed,
write **D** if this area is a **DELEGATED** power,
write **R** if it is a **RESERVED** power,
and write **C** if it is a **CONCURRENT** power.

_____ 63. maintain armed forces
_____ 64. establish schools
_____ 65. conduct elections
_____ 66. declare war
_____ 67. regulate state business
_____ 68. borrow money
_____ 69. maintain law and order
_____ 70. establish post offices

_____ 71. establish courts
_____ 72. charter banks
_____ 73. establish foreign policy
_____ 74. coin money
_____ 75. levy taxes
_____ 76. provide for public safety
_____ 77. make marriage laws
_____ 78. admit new states

Middle Grade Book of Social Studies Tests   Copyright ©2001 by Incentive Publications, Inc., Nashville, TN.

Find the correct word to complete each sentence.

19th

citizenship

electors

candidates

BALLOT

residency

political party

platform

election

polling place

absentee

register

20th

referendum

district

26TH

79. The _____ amendment allowed women to vote.

80. The _____ amendment to the Constitution lowered the voting age to 18.

81. The actual votes that determine the winner in a presidential election are cast by _____ .

82. A _____ is a location where people go to vote in their district.

83. A _____ requirement is a length of time someone must live in a state before being able to vote there.

84. A _____ is the list that a voter uses for the actual voting process.

85. An _____ ballot can be used by someone who cannot get to the polls on election day.

86. To officially sign up to vote is to _____ .

87. A _____ is a vote on a specific issue such as a city project or local issue.

88. People who are running for political offices are called _____ .

89. A _____ is a statement of a political party's policies and principles.

90. The place a citizen lives and is registered to vote is his or her voting _____ .

Middle Grade Book of Social Studies Tests

OFFICIALS, AGENCIES & INSTITUTIONS

Name _____   Possible Correct Answers: 45

Date _____   Your Correct Answers: _____

Circle the best answer.

1. . . . the Attorney General?
   a. at the Treasury Department
   b. in the Senate
   c. at the Department of Energy
   d. at the Justice Department

2. . . . a 30-year old representative
   elected to a six-year term?
   a. in the President's Cabinet
   b. in the Senate
   c. in the House of Representatives
   d. on the Supreme Court

3. . . . the Secretary of the Interior?
   a. decorating the White House
   b. at a meeting of the President's Cabinet
   c. at the CIA
   d. voting in the Senate

4. . . . someone issuing a veto
   a. in the Secretary of State's office
   b. at the Supreme Court
   c. in the oval office
   d. in the House of Representatives

5. . . . a life-time appointee?
   a. at the Department of State
   b. on the Supreme Court
   c. in the Senate
   d. in a state governor's office

6. . . . the mayor of Chicago?
   a. at a Chicago city council meeting
   b. in Illinois' Senate
   c. in Illinois' House of Representatives
   d. in the U.S. Senate

7. . . . the Chief of Staff?
   a. in the president's office
   b. at the State Department
   c. at the Department of Education
   d. in a governor's office

8. . . . the Secretary of Defense?
   a. at the U.S. Mint
   b. at the Pentagon
   c. at the Supreme Court
   d. in a U.S. Embassy

9. . . . the Ambassador to Brazil?
   a. at a Cabinet meeting
   b. in a state Capitol Building
   c. in a U.S. Embassy
   d. in the House of Representatives

On each newspaper, write the name of the president in office at the time of the headline.

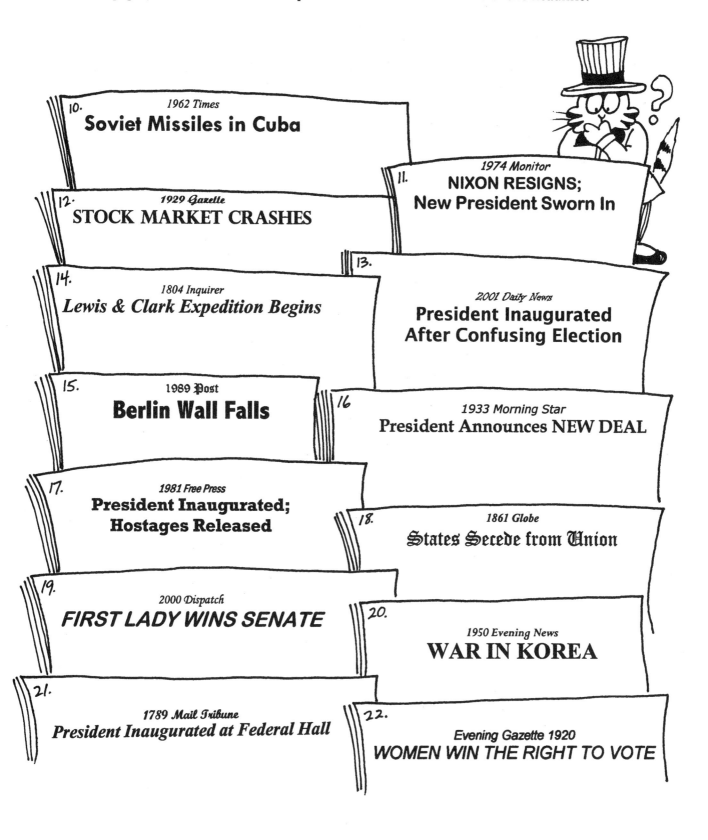

10. *1962 Times*
Soviet Missiles in Cuba

11. *1974 Monitor*
**NIXON RESIGNS;
New President Sworn In**

12. *1929 Gazette*
STOCK MARKET CRASHES

14. *1804 Inquirer*
Lewis & Clark Expedition Begins

13. *2001 Daily News*
**President Inaugurated
After Confusing Election**

15. *1989 Post*
Berlin Wall Falls

16. *1933 Morning Star*
President Announces NEW DEAL

17. *1981 Free Press*
**President Inaugurated;
Hostages Released**

18. *1861 Globe*
States Secede from Union

19. *2000 Dispatch*
FIRST LADY WINS SENATE

20. *1950 Evening News*
WAR IN KOREA

21. *1789 Mail Tribune*
President Inaugurated at Federal Hall

22. *Evening Gazette 1920*
WOMEN WIN THE RIGHT TO VOTE

Middle Grade Book of Social Studies Tests

23. Who is the chief executive officer of a state?

_____ *(name of position)*

24. Who is the chief executive officer of a city?

_____ *(name of position)*

25. What elected officials make decisions for a local school district?

_____ *(name of position)*

26. What elected officers make decisions for a county?

_____ *(name of position)*

27. What legislative body makes decisions for states? _____

28. What legislative body makes decisions for a town or city? _____

29. The largest museum complex in the world and a center for research and education is the

_____

30. Its primary purpose is to serve the Congress of the U.S., but all citizens can use its collection of resources and services. It is also official U.S. copyright agency. What is this institution?

_____

31. Which statement about governmental principles in the U.S. is NOT true?
(Circle one or more answers).

a. The institutions of all governments are founded on basic principles.

b. A basic principle of the U.S. government is *representative democracy*.

c. One of the democratic ideals of the U.S. government is the ideal of *popular sovereignty*, (meaning that the president whom the people elect has the ultimate government authority.)

d. One of the democratic ideals of the U.S. government is the belief in a *representative government* (meaning that the people delegate their powers to the elected officials.)

e. One of the democratic ideals of the U.S. government is the belief in *federalism*, (a system in which the federal government has authority over all state governments decisions.)

f. One of the democratic ideals of the U.S. government is the belief in a system of *checks and balances* as a part of the design of the government structure.

Middle Grade Book of Social Studies Tests

Match the government agency or corporation with the correct function.
Write the letters of the correct name on each line.

NASA		INS		BLM		CIA
IRS		BIA		SEC	
FCC		FAA		FDA		OSHA
	DEA		EPA		FDIC	

_____ 32. administers laws relating to administration and naturalization of aliens

_____ 33. regulates legal drug trade and tries to reduce the supply of illegal drugs

_____ 34. assures health and safety for workers on the job

_____ 35. gathers information to protect U.S. national security

_____ 36. monitors pollution and protects the environment

_____ 37. regulates financial markets

_____ 38. administrates policies for Native Americans

_____ 39. manages federal lands

_____ 40. collects federal taxes

_____ 41. operates federal space program

_____ 42. regulates communications companies

_____ 43. approves safety of food and drugs

_____ 44. insures bank deposits

_____ 45. regulates the airline industry

Middle Grade Book of Social Studies Tests

U.S. CITIZENSHIP

Name _____

Date _____

Possible Correct Answers: 45

Your Correct Answers: _____

KNOW YOUR GOVERNMENT!

1. Name the current U.S. president_____

2. Name one of your U.S. senators_____

3. Name your U.S. Representative to Congress_____

4. Name your state's governor_____

5. Name one of your state senators or representatives_____

6. Where is the center of government for your state?_____

7. Name the mayor or administrator of your town or city._____

8. Name one of your county's commissioners._____

9. Name one other local representative, such as a city council
   representative or a local school board member._____

10. Tell one important thing about the history of your state:

   _____

Middle Grade Book of Social Studies Tests   Copyright ©2001 by Incentive Publications, Inc., Nashville, TN.

Write the letter of the correct question next to the number of the answer.
(There are more questions than answers.)

A. *Who is the U. S. Vice-President?*

B. *What is the Constitution?*

C. *Who is the Secretary of State?*

D. *Who is the Chief Justice of the Supreme Court?*

E. *What is the Declaration of Independence?*

F. *What is the Electoral College?*

G. *What is a polling place?*

H. *What is voter turnout?*

I. *What is a ballot?*

J. *What is paying taxes?*

K. *What is registering?*

L. *What is age 18?*

M. *What is age 25?*

N. *What is an election?*

O. *What is a precinct?*

VOTE FOR ME—Aristotle!

Aristotle IS A RAT!

_____11. the process of voting for public officials

_____12. the smallest election district within a county

_____13. the tool used for placing a vote

_____14. the legal age for voting

_____15. a place where voting takes place

_____16. a responsibility of citizens

_____17. the document that protects the right of a U.S. citizen to vote

_____18. the youngest age a U.S. Representative to Congress can be

_____19. the body that actually places the final vote for the U.S. President

_____20. the person who administers the oath of office to the new U. S. President

_____21. the person who administers the oath of office to the new U. S. Senators

_____22. the number of eligible voters who actually vote in an election

_____23. what a citizen must do before she is able to vote in an election

Name _____

Middle Grade Book of Social Studies Tests

24. Aristotle visits a town where the Constitution and the Declaration of Independence were written. Where is he?

_____

25. Aristotle visits the Statue of Liberty. Where is he?

_____

26. Aristotle sits at the site where the wagon trains began their journey on the Oregon Trail. Where is he?

_____

I'm off to see America!

27. Aristotle sings the national anthem of the United States. What are the first 10 words?

_____

_____

28. Aristotle ponders an American flag. He counts the stripes. How many are there? ____

29. Aristotle visits the Liberty Bell. Where is he?_____

30. Aristotle visits the oldest city in the United States. Where is he? _____

31. Aristotle visits the site of the first U.S. capital. Where is he?_____

32. Aristotle walks the site of the Little Bighorn Battle. Where is he? _____

33. Aristotle looks at the official seal of the United States. What will he see on the seal?

_____

34. Aristotle visits a site where the faces of presidents are carved. Where is he?

_____

35. Aristotle stands on a bridge in the town where the first shots of the Revolutionary War were fired.

Where is he?_____

STOP

Middle Grade Book of Social Studies Tests

Copyright ©2001 by Incentive Publications, Inc., Nashville, TN.

KEEPING TRACK OF SKILLS

Student Progress Record 154

Class Progress Record
       (World Understandings, World Geography) 155

Class Progress Record
       (Map Skills, World History) 157

Class Progress Record
       (U.S. History, U.S. Government & Citizenship) 157

Good Skill Sharpeners for Social Studies 158

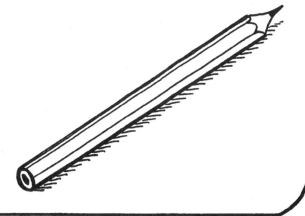

STUDENT PROGRESS RECORD — SOCIAL STUDIES SKILLS

Student Name _____

WORLD UNDERSTANDINGS TESTS	SCORE	COMMENTS & NEEDS
TEST DATE		
Test # 1 Social & Cultural Concepts & Relationships	of 55	
Test # 2 World Cultures	of 50	
Test # 3 Economics	of 45	

WORLD GEOGRAPHY TESTS	SCORE ____ OF ____	COMMENTS & NEEDS
TEST DATE		
Test # 1 Geographical Features	of 70	
Test # 2 World Regions	of 35	
Test # 3 Important Places & Spaces	of 70	
Test # 4 U.S. Geography	of 40	
Test # 5 Human Geography	of 35	

MAP SKILLS TESTS	SCORE ____ OF ____	COMMENTS & NEEDS
TEST DATE		
Test # 1 Map Tools & Resources	of 35	
Test # 2 Directions, Distances, & Locations	of 30	
Test # 3 Finding Information on Maps	of 30	

WORLD HISTORY TESTS	SCORE ____ OF ____	COMMENTS & NEEDS
TEST DATE		
Test # 1 Major Eras & Events	of 60	
Test # 2 People, Places, & Organizations	of 65	
Test # 3 Ancient World History	of 40	
Test # 4 Medieval & Modern History Through 1900	of 50	
Test # 5 Modern History Since 1900	of 55	

UNITED STATES HISTORY TESTS	SCORE ____ OF ____	COMMENTS & NEEDS
TEST DATE		
Test # 1 Major Eras & Events in U.S. History	of 50	
Test # 2 People, Places, & Organizations	of 55	
Test # 3 Early History (through 1900)	of 40	
Test # 4 19th Century History	of 40	
Test # 5 Modern History (since 1900)	of 50	

U.S. GOVERNMENT & CITIZENSHIP TESTS	SCORE ____ OF ____	COMMENTS & NEEDS
TEST DATE		
Test # 1 Key U.S. Documents	of 40	
Test # 2 Government Structure & Function	of 90	
Test # 3 Officials, Agencies, & Institutions	of 45	
Test # 4 U.S. Citizenship	of 35	

Middle Grade Book of Social Studies Tests

CLASS PROGRESS RECORD – SOCIAL STUDIES SKILLS

(World Understandings & World Geography)

Class _____

Teacher _____

WORLD UNDERSTANDINGS TESTS

TEST DATE	TEST	COMMENTS ABOUT RESULTS	SKILLS NEEDING RE-TEACHING
	Test # 1 Social & Cultural Concepts & Relationships		
	Test # 2 World Cultures		
	Test # 3 Economics		

WORLD GEOGRAPHY TESTS

TEST DATE	TEST	COMMENTS ABOUT RESULTS	SKILLS NEEDING RE-TEACHING
	Test # 1 Geographical Features		
	Test # 2 World Regions		
	Test # 3 Important Places & Spaces		
	Test # 4 U.S. Geography		
	Test # 5 Human Geography		

CLASS PROGRESS RECORD – SOCIAL STUDIES SKILLS
(Map Skills & World History)

Class _____   Teacher _____

MAP SKILLS TESTS

TEST DATE	TEST	COMMENTS ABOUT RESULTS	SKILLS NEEDING RE-TEACHING
	Test # 1 Map Tools & Resources		
	Test # 2 Directions, Distances, & Locations		
	Test # 3 Finding Information on Maps		

WORLD HISTORY TESTS

TEST DATE	TEST	COMMENTS ABOUT RESULTS	SKILLS NEEDING RE-TEACHING
	Test # 1 Major Eras & Events		
	Test # 2 People, Places, & Organizations		
	Test # 3 Ancient World History		
	Test # 4 Medieval & Modern History (through 1900)		
	Test # 5 Modern History Since 1900		

Middle Grade Book of Social Studies Tests

CLASS PROGRESS RECORD — SOCIAL STUDIES SKILLS

(U.S. History & U.S. Government & Citizenship)

Class _____

Teacher _____

U.S. HISTORY TESTS

TEST DATE	TEST	COMMENTS ABOUT RESULTS	SKILLS NEEDING RE-TEACHING
	Test # 1 Eras & Events		
	Test # 2 People, Places, & Organizations		
	Test # 3 Early History Through 1900		
	Test # 4 19th Century U.S. History		
	Test # 5 Modern History Since 1900		

U.S. GOVERNMENT & CITIZENSHIP TESTS

TEST DATE	TEST	COMMENTS ABOUT RESULTS	SKILLS NEEDING RE-TEACHING
	Test # 1 Key U.S. Documents		
	Test # 2 Government Structure & Function		
	Test # 3 Officials, Agencies, & Institutions		
	Test # 4 U.S. Citizenship		

GOOD SKILL SHARPENERS
FOR SOCIAL STUDIES

The tests in this book will identify student needs for practice, re-teaching or reinforcement of basic skills. Once those areas of need are known, then what? You and your students need to find some good ways to strengthen those skills.

The BASIC/Not Boring Skills Series, published by Incentive Publications (www.incentivepublications.com), offers 20 books to sharpen basic skills at the Grades 6–8 level. Five of these books are full of social studies exercises. The books cover these topics: World Geography, World History, U.S. History, Map Skills, and U.S. Government & Citizenship.

The pages of these books are student-friendly, clever, and challenging—guaranteed not to be boring! They cover a wide range of skills, including the skills assessed in this book of tests. A complete checklist of skills is available at the front of each book, complete with a reference list directing you to the precise pages for polishing those skills.

TEST IN THIS BOOK Middle Grade Book of Social Studies Tests	Pages in this Book	You will find pages to sharpen skills in these locations from the BASIC/Not Boring Skills Series, published by Incentive Publications.
World Understandings Test # 1 **Social & Cultural Concepts & Relationships**	12–17	Gr. 6–8 World Geography
World Understandings Test # 2 **World Cultures**	18–23	Gr. 6–8 World Geography
World Understandings Test # 3 **Economics**	24–29	Gr. 6–8 U.S. Government, Economics, & Citizenship
World Geography Test # 1 **Geographical Features**	33–37	Gr. 6–8 World Geography
World Geography Test # 2 **World Regions**	38–41	Gr. 6–8 World Geography
World Geography Test # 3 **Important Places & Spaces**	42–47	Gr. 6–8 World Geography
World Geography Test # 4 **U.S. Geography**	48–51	Gr. 6–8 World Geography
World Geography Test # 5 **Human Geography**	52–55	Gr. 6–8 World Geography

(continued on next page)

GOOD SKILL SHARPENERS
FOR SOCIAL STUDIES

TEST IN THIS BOOK Middle Grade Book of Social Studies Tests	Pages in this Book	You will find pages to sharpen skills in these locations from the BASIC/Not Boring Skills Series, published by Incentive Publications.
Map Skills Test # 1 **Map Tools & Resources**	58–61	Gr. 6–8 Map Skills Gr. 6–8 World Geography
Map Skills Test # 2 **Directions, Distances, & Locations**	62–65	Gr. 6–8 Map Skills Gr. 6–8 World Geography
Map Skills Test # 3 **Finding Information on Maps**	66–71	Gr. 6–8 Map Skills Gr. 6–8 World Geography
World History Test # 1 **Major Eras & Events**	75-81	Gr. 6–8 World History
World History Test # 2 **People, Places, & Organizations**	82-87	Gr. 6–8 World History
World History Test # 3 **Ancient World History**	88-93	Gr. 6–8 World History
World History Test # 4 **Medieval & Modern History (through 1900)**	94-99	Gr. 6–8 World History
World History Test # 5 **Modern History Since 1900**	100-105	Gr. 6–8 World History
U.S. History Test # 1 **Major Eras & Events**	109-113	Gr. 6–8 U.S. History Gr. 6–8 U.S. Government, Economics, & Citizenship
U.S. History Test # 2 **People, Places, & Organizations**	114-119	Gr. 6–8 U.S. History Gr. 6–8 U.S. Government, Economics, & Citizenship
U.S. History Test # 3 **Early History Through 1900**	120-123	Gr. 6–8 U.S. History Gr. 6–8 U.S. Government, Economics, & Citizenship

(continued on next page)

Middle Grade Book of Social Studies Tests

GOOD SKILL SHARPENERS
FOR SOCIAL STUDIES

TEST IN THIS BOOK Middle Grade Book of Social Studies Tests	Pages in this Book	You will find pages to sharpen skills in these locations from the BASIC/Not Boring Skills Series, published by Incentive Publications.
U.S. History Test # 4 **19th Century History**	124-127	Gr. 6–8 U.S. History Gr. 6–8 U.S. Government, Economics, & Citizenship
U.S. History Test # 5 **Major Eras & Events**	128-133	Gr. 6–8 U.S. History Gr. 6–8 U.S. Government, Economics, & Citizenship
U. S. Government & Citizenship Test # 1 **Key U.S. Documents**	136-139	Gr. 6–8 U.S. Government, Economics, & Citizenship Gr. 6–8 U.S. History
U. S. Government & Citizenship Test # 2 **Government Structure & Function**	140-145	Gr. 6–8 U.S. Government, Economics, & Citizenship Gr. 6–8 U.S. History
U. S. Government & Citizenship Test # 3 **Officials, Agencies, & Organizations**	146-149	Gr. 6–8 U.S. Government, Economics, & Citizenship Gr. 6–8 U.S. History
U. S. Government & Citizenship Test # 4 **U. S. Citizenship**	150-152	Gr. 6–8 U.S. Government, Economics, & Citizenship

ANSWER KEYS

World Understandings Answer Key 162–163

World Geography Answer Key 164–165

Map Skills Answer Key 166–167

World History Answer Key 168–170

U.S. History Answer Key 171–172

U.S. Government & Citizenship Answer Key 173–174

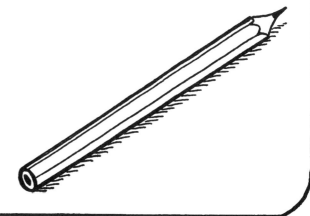

WORLD UNDERSTANDINGS TESTS
ANSWER KEY

Cultural Concepts & Relationships (Test on page 12)

1. e
2. d
3. a
4. a
5. d
6. d
7. j
8. q
9. f
10. l
11. a
12. k
13. p
14. i
15. b
16. h
17. r
18. e
19. m
20. o

21. c
22. n
23. g
24. a
25. e
26. a, b, c, e
27. c
28. b
9-38: Students may choose
one of the answers
listed.
29. B, C, F, K, M, or N
30. B, C, D, G, K, M, or N
31. D, F, K, M, O, or N
32. C or M
33. C, F, G, K, or N
34. E, F, G, I, J, or K
35. A, B, C, F, or M
36. F, G, or N
37. E, F, G, H, I, or J

38. E, F, or L
39. b, c, d, f
40. a
41. a
42. b
43. c
44. c
45. c
46. b
47. b
48. B
49. C
50. H
51. E
52. A
53. F
54. D
55. G

World Cultures (Test on page 18)

1. b
2. a
3. b
4. c
5. b
6. a
7. b
8. F
9. B
10. A
11. D
12. G
13. H
14. E
15. I
16. C
17. b

18. b
19. b
20. b
21. d
22. a
23. b
24. c
25. F
26. C
27. B
28. D
29. H
30. G
31. J
32. A
33. I
34. E

35. a
36. b
37. c
38. d
39. e
40. d
41. c
42. Sub-Saharan Africa
43. Middle East
44. Antarctica
45. European Community
46. Arabic
47. Eastern Europe
48. Pakistan
49. apartheid
50. China

Middle Grade Book of Social Studies Tests
Copyright ©2001 by Incentive Publications, Inc., Nashville, TN.

WORLD UNDERSTANDINGS TESTS
ANSWER KEY

Economics (Test on page 24)

1. A, C, F
2. a
3. c
4. b
5. c
6. c
7. a
8. Answers may vary.
   Costs: loss of newer, fancier cycle, fewer features, loss of prestige
   Benefits: saved money on price, save money on interest
9. a, d, f, g, k
10. b, d, e, i, j
11. a, b, e
12. a, c, d
13. a
14. c
15. b
16. c
17. d
18. a
19. b, c, e
20. interest, prospect of getting a car in the future
21. getting a CD player now, friends having CD player, magazine ad
22. c
23. diversified
24. exempt
25. resources
26. corporation
27. investment
28. subsistence
29. entrepreneur
30. unearned (or interest)
31. Interest
32. Earned
33. capital
34. embargo
35. depression
36. competition
37. wants
38. Inflation
39. profit
40. recession (or depression)
41. consumer
42. Needs
43. demand
44. producer
45. credit

Middle Grade Book of Social Studies Tests

WORLD GEOGRAPHY TESTS
ANSWER KEY

Geographical Features (Test on page 33)

1. P
2. C
3. C
4. P
5. P
6. C
7. C
8. P
9. C
10. C
11. P
12. P
13. P
14. C
15. P
16. P
17. revolution
18. fall
19. 4
20. J
21. C
22. R
23. O
24. B
25. G
26. Q
27. P
28. I
29. K
30. H
31. N
32. D
33. L
34. M
35. E
36. A
37. F
38. peninsula
39. source
40. archipelago
41. seamount
42. delta
43. gulf
44. cape
45. glacier
46. cliff
47. canyon
48. isthmus
49. plateau
50. b, d, e, g, h
51. a, b, d
52. b, d, g, h, i, j
53. a
54. b
55. Europe
56. South America
57. South America, Asia, or Africa
58. c
59. b
60. b
61–70.: The following answers are correct and should be circled: 61, 63, 64, 66, 68, 69, 70

World Regions (Test on page 38)

1. a, b
2. a, c, f
3. a, c, d, e
4. c, d
5. b, c
6. a, d, f
7. a, d
8. a, c, d
9. South America
10. The Pacific
11. Middle East & North Africa
12. Eastern Europe & Russia
13. Middle America or Central America
14. Western Europe
15. Eastern and Southern Asia
16. North America
17. Sub-Saharan Africa
18. SSA
19. NA
20. WE
21. P
22. EE
23. SA
24. AS
25. ME
26. MA
27. c
28. a
29. a
30. b, c
31. a, b
32. a
33. b, d
34. b
35. b, c

Middle Grade Book of Social Studies Tests
Copyright ©2001 by Incentive Publications, Inc., Nashville, TN.

WORLD GEOGRAPHY TESTS
ANSWER KEY

Important Places & Spaces (Test on page 42)

1. Atlantic Ocean, Brazil
2. Mediterranean Sea, Africa
3. Atlantic Ocean, Europe
4. North America and Europe
5. Northern, Southern, Eastern
6. Asia
7. South America, Africa, Asia, or Antarctica
8. Nicaragua
9. Haiti
10. Panama
11. Venezuela
12. Ecuador
13. Peru
14. Argentina
15. Paraguay
16. b, d, e
17. c, d
18. a, b, d, f
19. H
20. M
21. P
22. C
23. D
24. T
25. F
26. J
27. A
28. S
29. G
30. N
31. K
32. E
33. Malaysia
34. Korea
35. Cuba
36. Hungary
37. Italy
38. China
39. Egypt
40. Austria
41. Australia
42. Bolivia
43. Canada
44. Ecuador
45. India
46. Venezuela
47. Germany
48. Mexico
49. Brazil
50. South Africa
51. United Kingdom or Northern Ireland
52. Sweden
53. Laos, Burma, Vietnam, Malaysia, Cambodia
54. Sacramento, Damascus
55. Johannesburg
56. Sri Lanka
57. Madrid
58. Greenland
59. Poland, Austria, Netherlands
60. Ghana, Zambia, Congo, Kenya
61. Nepal
62. Romania
63. b
64. c
65. c
66. b
67. North America
68. Asia
69. Africa
70. Europe

United States Geography (Test on page 48)

1. b
2. d
3. b
4. a
5. g
6. G
7. H
8. M
9. Q
10. A
11. J
12. F
13. L
14. N
15. P
16. C
17. D
18. I
19. T
20. K
21. X
22. V
23. S
24. B or Louisiana
25. E or Washington
26. R or Pennsylvania
27. b
28. b
29. c
30. a
31. c
32. a
33. a
34. b
35. Gigi
36. Spike
37. Spike
38. Aristotle
39. Spike
40. B, C

Human Geography (Test on page 52)

1. d
2. b
3. e
4. a, d, e
5. b
6. c
7. c
8. b
9. 0
10. 4
11. 8
12. Bombay
13. New York
14. U.S.A.
15. Italy
16. Great Britain, United Kingdom, or England
17. China
18. France
19. Great Britain, United Kingdom, or England
20. Panama
21. Egypt
22. India
23. Italy
24. anthropologist
25. megalopolis
26. Commonwealth
27. demographics
28. autonomy
29. ethnic
30. nomads
31. arable
32. Population density
33. separatists
34. irrigation
35. standard of living

Middle Grade Book of Social Studies Tests

MAP SKILLS ANSWER KEY

Map Tools & Resources (Test on page 58)

1. a
2. d
3. 105 mi
4. a
5. scale
6. title
7. key
8. 4
9. 7 (or 8)
10. c
11. T
12. F
13. F
14. T
15. Northern
16. Western
17. Southern
18. Eastern
19. North Pole, 90° N
20. Arctic Circle, 66° N
21. Tropic of Cancer, 23½ ° N
22. equator, 0°
23. Tropic of Capricorn, 23½ ° S
24. Antarctic Circle, 66° S
25. South Pole, 90° S
26. c
27. a
28. d
29. c
30. c
31. H5 or H6
32. E3
33. E9
34. G2 or G3
35. B7

Directions, Distances, & Locations (Test on page 62)

1. d
2. Rogue Island
3. Smuggler's Island
4. c
5. b
6. NE
7. SE
8. S
9. E or NE
10. E
11. SW
12. a
13. b
14. c
15. Beijing
16. Mediterranean Sea
17. Dakar
18. Nairobi
19. Damascus
20. Oslo
21. Indian Ocean
22. Tokyo
23. Greenwich
24. St. Petersburg
25. C
26. H
27. D
28. B
29. G
30. M

Middle Grade Book of Social Studies Tests

MAP SKILLS ANSWER KEY

Finding Information on Maps (Test on page 66)

1. Rt 30, Rt 89
2. a, c, d
3. c
4. b
5. Ontario
6. Nova Scotia, Prince Edward Island
7. Vancouver
8. 3
9. 1600 Ft
10. 2200 ft
11. 200 ft
12. 600 ft
13. 400 ft
14. 150
15. 550
16. 825 gecko
17. Little Gecko Island
18. 825
19. 200 geckos
20. 12:00 p.m.
21. 11:00 p.m.
22. 9:30 a.m.
23. 2:10 p.m.
24. c
25. 10-20 inches
26. 20-40 inches
27. 17
28. Vera Cruz, Tampico
29. 4
30. LaPaz

Middle Grade Book of Social Studies Tests

WORLD HISTORY ANSWER KEY

Major Events & Eras in World History (Test on page 75)

1. E
2. F
3. N
4. C
5. A
6. L
7. B
8. D
9–18. Answers may vary.
9. beginning of Renaissance
10. one cause of World War I
11. civil war tears Yugoslavia apart after fall of the communist government
12. host Olympics
13. conference dividing of Europe at the end of World War II
14. U.S. drops atomic bombs on Japan to end World War II
15. Israel established
16. Soviet Union breaks up making way for non-communist countries in Eastern Europe
17. Berlin Wall built; it is a symbolic beginning of the Cold War
18. space race begins
19. d
20. b
21. b
22. a
23. c
24. b
25. d
26. b
27. d
28. b
29. b
30. a
31. d
32. b
33. d
34. a
34. b
36. a
37. c
38. a
39. d
40. d
41. c, d
42. b, c
43. H
44. B
45. D
46. A
47. E
48. C
49. G
50. F
51. Pax Romana
52. republic
53. perestroika
54. civil war
55. mosque
56. feudalism
57. apartheid
58. caste
59–60: Answers will vary; make sure students give two clear explanations

People, Places, & Organizations (Test on page 82)

1. I
2. P
3. W or N
4. X or T
5. V
6. M or E
7. O
8. S
9. U
10. Y, C, or H
11. L
12. K
13. R
14. B
15. J
16. F
17. Z
18. A
19. Martin Luther
20. Michelangelo
21. Winston Churchill
22. Shakespeare
23. Moses
24. Magellan
25. Karl Marx
26. Ghandi
27. Joan of Arc
28. James Watt
29. E
30. G
31. M
32. A
33. N
34. I
35. C
36. J
37. D
38. L
39. H
40. B
41. K
42. F
43. Northern Ireland
44. Australia
45. Kuwait
46. Lance
47. Poland
48. England (Great Britain, or UK)
49. Iran
50. b
51. OPEC
52. UN
53. IMF
54. WHO
55. UNICEF
56. EC
57. PLO
58. UNESCO
59. c
60. a
61. c
62. b
63. b
64. a
65. a

Middle Grade Book of Social Studies Tests

WORLD HISTORY ANSWER KEY

Ancient World History (Test on page 88)

1. b	21. H
2. b	22. B
3. c	23. b
4. c	24. c, f, h
5. B	25. b
6. C	26. c
7. A	27. a
8. c is the correct answer	28. city-state
9. answer is correct	29. Tigris and Euphrates
10. answer is correct	30. c
11. c is the correct answer	31. d
12. answer is correct	32. d
13. answer is correct	33. b
14. J	34. c
15. F	35. e
16. E	36. C
17. D	37. A
18. I	38. B
19. C	39. d
20. G	40. b

Medieval & Modern World History (Test on page 94)

1. a, b, c, e, f, g, h	22. d
2. b, c, d, e	23. Portugal
3. a, b, c, e, f	24. Spain
4. C	25. Britain
5. E	26. France
6. A	27. G
7. F	28. M
8. G	29. A
9. B	30. E
10. D	31. D
11. 1848	32. B
12. 1095	33. N
13. 1292	34. J
14. 1517	35. L
15. 1776	36. H
16. 1347	37. C
17. 2789	38. I
18. 1492	39. F
19. 800	40–50. The correctly-answered questions are
20. b	43, 45, 47, 48, 49
21. a, b, c, d	

Middle Grade Book of Social Studies Tests

WORLD HISTORY & U.S. HISTORY ANSWER KEY

Modern World History (Test on page 100)

1.- 12. Answers will vary. These are possible explanations:

1. The Communist government opened fire on student protesters to stop dissent toward the government; many students were killed.
2. The policy of racial discrimination that separated races in South Africa. Citizens fought for years to overturn this.
3. Time in 1960s in China when the government of Mao Zedong pressed to make all sectors of the society line up with communist ideals
4. a trade agreement allowing for free trade between the US, Canada, and Mexico
5. a wall built between East and West Berlin after World War I, symbolizing the Cold War division of democratic and communist countries
6. Russia launched the first space ship to orbit Earth, starting the space race between the USA and USSR

7. Japan bombed US ships in Hawaii, bringing the US into World War II
8. Arab terrorists killed Israeli athletes
9. The USA's CIA tried a plan to assassinate Castro in Cuba; the plan failed10. The Berlin Wall torn down-a symbol of the fall of communism in Eastern Europe
11. Iran took hostages in the U.S. Embassy in Tehran in an act of terrorism against the USA. The hostages were held for over a year.
12. Hitler's program to exterminate millions of Jews-one of the worst acts in human history

13. E
14. C
15. F
16. B
17. A
18. G
19. D
20. N
21. K
22. M
23. L
24. I

25. H
26. O
27. J
28. d
29. a
30. d
31. b
32. d
33. a, b
34. b
35. b
36. c
37. a, c, d
38. e
39. a, e
40. c
41. b, e
42. c, e
43. D
44. F
45. A
46. H
47. C
48. G
49. E
50. J
51. B
52. I
53. a
54. a
55. a

Major Eras & Events in U.S. History (Test on page 109)

1–8: Answers will vary. Students should write a short statement about eight of the items. Answers may be similar to these:

A. Underground Railroad
B. U-2 Affair
C. Monroe Doctrine
D. Bill of Rights
E. The Confederacy
F. Louisiana Purchase
G. Pearl Harbor
H. Cuban Missile Crisis
I. Election 2000
J. Black Tuesday

K. The Roaring Twenties
L. Trail of Rears
M. Arab Oil Crisis 1973
N. Salem Witch Trials
O. Gold Rush

9. c, d
10. c
11. b
12. C
13. E
14. A
15. F
16. H
17. J
18. B
19. D
20. I
21. G

22. a, b, c
23. a
24. a, b, c
25. a, b
26. a, b, c, d
27. a, b
28. H
29. B
30. C
31. A
32. G
33. D
34. E
35. F
36. J
37. B
38. J
39. D

40. I
41. F
42. C
43. G
44. E
45. H
46. a
47. d
48. a
49–50. Answers will vary. Check to see that student has written a clear explanation for two of the choices.

170

U.S. HISTORY ANSWER KEY

People, Places, & Organizations (Test on page 114)

1. Sandra Day O'Connor
2. Robert Oppenheimer
3. Jane Addams
4. Neil Armstrong
5. carpetbaggers
6. Susan B. Anthony
7. Joseph McCarthy
8. Franklin D. Roosevelt
9. Frances Perkins
10. Rosa Parks
11. Sacagewa, Davy Crockett, Meriwether Lewis
12. John D. Rockefeller, Samuel Gompers, Henry Ford, Huey Long, Andrew Carnegie
13. Harriet Beecher Stowe, Ulysses S. Grant, Harriet Tubman, Stephen Douglas, Dred Scott
14. William Bradford, Ethan Allen, Betsy Ross, Benedict Arnold, George Washington, William Penn, Thomas Paine
15. Josef Stalin, John F. Kennedy, Fidel Castro, Joseph McCarthy, Nikita Khrushchev, Winston Churchill
16. b
17. c
18. HI
19. AK
20. WY
21. UT
22. AR
23. MO
24. OR
25. VA
26. CA
27. NV
28. MT
29. MA
30. LA
31. PA
32. a
33. b
34. e
35. b
36. c
37. b
38. NAACP
39. CIA
40. AFL-CIO
41. AIM
42. KKK
43. EPA
44. TVA
45. FDIC
46. NATO
47. NASA
48. NOW
49. Peace Corps
50. a
51. b
52. b
53. c
54. a
55. c

Early U.S. History (Test on page 120)

1. T
2. F
3. T
4. T
5. F
6. F
7. F
8. F
9. T
10. T
11. F
12. T
13. F
14. T
15. Massachusetts
16. Delaware
17. Rhode Island
18. Pennsylvania
19. Georgia
20. New York
21. a
22. b
23. a
24. c
25. e
26. e
27. a
28–30: Answers may vary. Here is the general idea for each:
28. Famous words from a speech by Patrick Henry from Virginia urging resistance to the British.
29. When the British Parliament sent troops to Massachusetts to arrest the leaders of the Minute Men, Patriots tried to warn throughout the countryside that the British soldiers (the redcoats, as they were called) were coming.
30. The shots heard round the world were those that began the Revolutionary War when British troops and American Minute Men clashed in Lexington, leaving several Americans dead or wounded.
31. Answer may vary. In general, unalienable rights are rights that persons have just because they are human. These are not rights that are given or can be taken away by anyone.
32. d
33. G
34. F
35. B
36. H
37. A
38. C
39. E
40. D

Middle Grade Book of Social Studies Tests

U.S. HISTORY ANSWER KEY

19th Century U.S. History (Test on page 124)

1.–8: Answers will vary somewhat. General information below:

1. Gold Rush: thousands of people went to California in the late 1840s to look for gold. This increased numbers of people moving west, and added to development of the West.

2. Erie Canal: New York waterway that connected the Hudson River to Lake Erie and made commerce and travel easier between the East and Midwest

3. Lincoln-Douglas Debates: debates between the two Illinois senatorial candidates in the 1858 election. The debated highlighted the nation's division over the issues of slavery and abolition.

4. Homestead Act: Law passed in 1862 giving free public land to farmers who agreed to farm the land for a specific period of time

5. Lewis & Clark Expedition: President Jefferson's plan to explore the recently-purchased territory of the Louisiana Purchase. He sent the two explorers to map and describe the area, collect specimens, and find a water connection across the continent.

6. Louisiana Purchase: land purchase from France of all the land between the Mississippi River and the Rocky Mountains

7. Manifest Destiny: Attitude of Americans in the mid 1800s that it was the destiny of the people of the United States to spread over the whole continent

8. Monroe Doctrine: foreign policy statement by President Monroe that the U.S. would not allow European powers to interfere in the Western Hemisphere; this signaled a move of strength in world foreign policy

9. B
10. K
11. H
12. C
13. M
14. A
15. D
16. G or I
17. J
18. F
19. G
20. E or A
21. L
22. a, b, c, e
23. a, c, e, f,
24. a, b, c, e, f, g
25. c
26. b
27. a
28. b, c, d, f
29. b, c, d, e, f
30-31. Answers will vary; make sure student has given a good, accurate answer for each.
32. C
33. D
34. G
35. A
36. E
37. H
38. I
39. B
40. F

Middle Grade Book of Social Studies Tests

U.S. HISTORY ANSWER KEY

Modern U.S. History (Test on page 128)

1–7. Answers will vary. Students must write about seven of the items listed here.

Panama Canal: waterway across the isthmus of Panama which connected the Atlantic and Pacific Oceans, making travel faster

Stock Market Crash—1929 beginning of Great Depression

Bonus March—march of World War I veterans on Washington to protest the government's decision not to compensate in cash for their low pay during the war

Sacco-Vanzetti Case—case of extreme fear of foreigners after World War I—two foreigners were found guilty of murder with little evidence

D-Day—the beginning of the Allied invasion of France to drive Hitler out

Containment Policy—U.S. plan in the Cold War period to keep communism from spreading

Domino Theory—U.S. belief that if one country fell to communism, all the neighboring countries would also fall

SALT Treaties—agreements between U.S. and U.S.S.R to reduce nuclear weapons

Iran-Contra Affair—situation during Reagan administration where U.S. government secretly agreed to trade arms to Iran for the release of hostages

Watergate Affair—burglary of the Democratic Party's headquarters by Republicans before the 1972 election; scandal ended with Nixon's resigning

Wounded Knee—South Dakota site where Sioux Indians were massacred

Kent State University—Ohio university where students were killed during a protest of the Vietnam War

8. E
9. B
10. b
11. a
12. Austria-Hungary, Turkey, Germany, Bulgaria
13. b, c, d, e,
14. b

15. d
16. e
17. c
18. Drug Enforcement Agency. Environmental Protection Agency, National Farm Workers Association, Peace Corps
19. Britain, U.S.S.R., France, China, U.S.
20. Nato, Berlin Airlift, McCarthyism, U-2 Affair, Korean War, Berlin Wall, Tet Offensive, Vietnam War, Domino Theory, Launch of Sputnik, Bay of Pigs Invasion, Truman Doctrine, Cuban Missile Crisis, Policy of Containment, Berlin Blockade (optional: Marshall Plan)
21. b
22. c
23. a
24. c
25. d
26. b
27. True
28. True
29. False
30. True
31. True
32. False
33. False
34. False
35. True
36. False
37. E
38. B
39. A
40. C
41. D
42. G
43. F
44. I
45. J
46. H
47. b
48. a
49. c
50. b

U.S. GOVERNMENT & CITIZENSHIP
ANSWER KEY

Key U.S. Documents (Test on page 136)

1. A
2. BR
3. D
4. BR
5. G
6. AR
7. AR
8. P
9. D
10. rights that cannot be taken away; people have them automatically just because they are human
11. life, liberty, pursuit of happiness
12. D
13. D
14. G
15. BR
16. AR
17. G
18. A
19. P
20. BR
21. AR
22. c, d
23. right to a speedy trial
24. right of free speech
25. protection from being charged with the same crime twice
26. protection from cruel and unusual punishments
27. right to bear arms
28. protection from unreasonable search
29. AR
30. BR
31. A
32. AR
33. AR
34. AR
35. freedom from slavery, right to be citizens, right to vote
36. production or sale of alcohol
37. voting age
38. right to vote
39. president cannot serve more than 2 terms
40. gave the government the right to tax citizens (with an income tax)

Middle Grade Book of Social Studies Tests

U.S. GOVERNMENT & CITIZENSHIP ANSWER KEY

Government Structure & Function (Test on page 140)

1. A. executive, legislative, judicial
   B. each branch has different powers so no one branch has all the power
2. a
3. d
4. d
5. d
6. U.S. Representative to Congress
7. C
8. C
9. H
10. C
11. P
12. SC
13. P
14. S
15. S
16. S
17. P
18. P
19. Secretary of State
20. Secretary of Education
21. Secretary of Housing and Urban Development
22. Secretary of Labor
23. Secretary of the Treasury
24. Attorney General
25. Secretary of Veterans' Affairs
26. Secretary of the Interior
27. Secretary of Defense
28. Secretary of Commerce
29. Secretary of Education
30. Secretary of Agriculture
31–41: The following numbers should be circled: 31, 32, 33, 34, 38, 39
42. The order is: 5, 2, 6, 7, 3, 4, 1
43. Congress can override the veto with a vote of $2/3$ majorities in both houses
44. Cross out 9; replace with 13.
45. Cross out Senate; replace with president. Cross out president, replace with Senate.
46. Cross out no; replace with 2.
47. Cross out four; replace with five.
48. Cross out cannot be removed. Replace with can be removed.
49. Cross out passes laws; replace with decides the constitutionality of laws.
50. Cross out appeals court; replace with Supreme Court.
51. Cross out 12 years; replace with life.
52. A
53. F
54. C
55. G
56. B
57. D
58. F
59. E
60. B
61. C
62. A
63. D
64. R
65. C
66. D
67. R
68. C
69. C
70. D
71. C
72. C
73. D
74. D
75. C
76. R
77. R
78. D
79. 19th
80. 26th
81. electors
82. polling place (or district)
83. residency
84. ballot
85. absentee
86. register
87. referendum
88. candidates
89. platform
90. district

U.S. GOVERNMENT & CITIZENSHIP
ANSWER KEY

Officials, Agencies, & Institutions (Test on page 146)

1. d	16. Franklin D. Roosevelt	31. c, e
2. b	17. Ronald Reagan	32. INS
3. b	18. Abraham Lincoln	33. DEA
4. c	19. William Clinton	34. OSHA
5. b	20. Harry Truman	35. CIA
6. a	21. George Washington	36. EPA
7. a	22. Woodrow Wilson	37. SEC
8. b	23. governor	38. BIA
9. c	24. mayor	39. BLM
10. John F. Kennedy	25. school board members	40. IRS
11. Gerald Ford	26. county commissioners	41. NASA
12. Herbert Hoover	27. state legislature	42. FCC
13. George W. Bush	28. town or city council	43. FDA
14. Thomas Jefferson	29. Smithsonian Institute	44. FDIC
15. George H. Bush	30. Library of Congress	45. FAA

Citizenship (Test on page 150)

1–10. Answers will vary. Check them for accuracy.	24. Philadelphia
11. N	25. New York City
12. O	26. Missouri (or St. Louis)
13. I	27. "O say can you see by the dawn's early light?"
14. L	28. 13
15. G or O	29. Philadelphia
16. J	30. St. Petersburg, FL
17. B	31. New York City
18. M	32. Montana
19. F	33. Either of these: American Eagle, e pluribus unum
20. D	34. Mt. Rushmore
21. A	35. Lexington MA, (or Concord)
22. H	
23. K	

Middle Grade Book of Social Studies Tests